GOING TO EXTREMES

Going to Extremes

How Like Minds Unite and Divide

Cass R. Sunstein

OXFORD
UNIVERSITY PRESS

2009

OXFORD
UNIVERSITY PRESS

Oxford University Press, Inc., publishes works that further
Oxford University's objective of excellence
in research, scholarship, and education.

Oxford New York
Auckland Cape Town Dar es Salaam Hong Kong Karachi
Kuala Lumpur Madrid Melbourne Mexico City Nairobi
New Delhi Shanghai Taipei Toronto

With offices in
Argentina Austria Brazil Chile Czech Republic France Greece
Guatemala Hungary Italy Japan Poland Portugal Singapore
South Korea Switzerland Thailand Turkey Ukraine Vietnam

Copyright © 2009 by Cass R. Sunstein

Published by Oxford University Press, Inc.
198 Madison Avenue, New York, NY 10016

www.oup.com

Oxford is a registered trademark of Oxford University Press

Library of Congress Cataloging-in-Publication Data
Sunstein, Cass R.
Going to extremes : how like minds unite and divide / Cass R. Sunstein.
     p. cm.
Includes bibliographical references and index.
ISBN 978-0-19-537801-6
   1. Extremists—United States.   2. Radicalism—United States.   I. Title.
HN90.R3S848 2009
303.48'40973—dc22   2008043339

9 8 7 6 5 4 3 2 1

Printed in the United States of America
on acid-free paper

For Samantha

Contents

CHAPTER 1

Polarization

What explains the rise of fascism in the 1930s? The emergence of student radicalism in the 1960s? The growth of Islamic terrorism in the 1990s? The Rwandan genocide in 1994? Ethnic conflict in the former Yugoslavia and in Iraq? Acts of torture and humiliation by American soldiers at Abu Ghraib prison? The American financial crisis of 2008? The widespread belief, in some parts of the world, that Israel or the United States was responsible for the attacks of September 11, 2001? And what, if anything, do these questions have to do with one another?

Here is a clue. Some years ago, a number of citizens of France were assembled into small groups to exchange views about their president and about the intentions of the United States with respect to foreign aid.[1] Before they started to talk, the participants tended to like their president and to distrust the intentions of the United States. After they talked, some strange things happened. Those who began by liking their president ended up liking their president significantly more. And those who expressed mild distrust toward the United States moved in the direction of far greater distrust. The small groups of French citizens became more extreme. As a result of their discussions, they were more enthusiastic about their leader, and far more skeptical of the United States, than similar people in France who had not been brought together to speak with one another.

This tale reveals a general fact of social life: Much of the time, groups of people end up thinking and doing things that group members would never think or do on their own. This is true for groups of teenagers, who are willing to run risks that individuals would avoid. It is certainly true for those prone to violence, including terrorists and those who commit genocide. It is true for investors and corporate executives. It is true for government officials, neighborhood groups, social reformers, political protestors, police officers, student organizations, labor unions, and juries. Some of the best and worst developments in social life are a product of group dynamics, in which members of organizations, both small and large, move one another in new directions.

Of course, the best explanations of fascism are not adequate to explain student rebellions, and even if we understand both of these, we will not be able to explain ethnic conflict in Iraq, the Rwandan genocide, abuse and brutality at Abu Ghraib, conspiracy theories involving Israel, or the subprime crisis. For particular events, general explanations can uncover only parts of the picture. But I do aim to show striking similarities among a wide range of social phenomena. The unifying theme is simple: *When people find themselves in groups of like-minded types, they are especially likely to move to extremes.* And when such groups include authorities who tell group members what to do, or who put them into certain social roles, very bad things can happen.

In exploring why this is so, I hope to see what might be done about unjustified extremism—a threat to security, to peace, to economic development, and to sensible decisions in all sorts of domains. My emphasis throughout is on the phenomenon of *group polarization*. This phenomenon offers large lessons about the behavior of consumers, interest groups, the real estate market, religious organizations, political parties, liberation movements, executive agencies, legislatures, racists, judicial panels, those who make peace, those who make war, and even nations as a whole.

GROUPS AND EXTREMISM

When people talk together, what happens? Do group members compromise? Do they move toward the middle of the tendencies of their individual members? The answer is now clear, and it is not what intuition would suggest: Groups go to extremes. More precisely, members of a deliberating group usually end up at a more extreme position in the same general direction as their inclinations before deliberation began.[2]

This is the phenomenon known as group polarization. Group polarization is the typical pattern with deliberating groups. It is not limited to particular periods, nations, or cultures. On the contrary, group polarization has been found in hundreds of studies involving more than a dozen countries, including the United States, France, Afghanistan, New Zealand, Taiwan, and Germany.[3] It provides a clue to extremism of many different kinds.

Consider four examples:

1. White people who tend to show significant racial prejudice will show more racial prejudice after speaking with one another. By contrast, white people who

tend to show little racial prejudice will show less prejudice after speaking with one another.[4]

2. Feminism becomes more attractive to women after they talk to one another—at least if the women who are talking begin with an inclination in favor of feminism.[5]

3. Those who approve of an ongoing war effort, and think that the war is going well, become still more enthusiastic about that effort, and still more optimistic, after they talk together.

4. If investors begin with the belief that it is always best to invest in real estate, their eagerness to invest in real estate will grow as a result of discussions with one another.

In these and countless other cases, like-minded people tend to move to a more extreme version of what they thought before they started to talk. Suppose in this light that enclaves of people are inclined to rebellion or even violence and that they are separated from other groups. They might move sharply in the direction of violence as a consequence of their self-segregation. Political extremism is often a product of group polarization,[6] and social segregation is a useful tool for producing polarization.

In fact, a good way to create an extremist group, or a cult of any kind, is to separate members from the rest of society. The separation can occur physically or psychologically, by creating a sense of suspicion about nonmembers. With such separation, the information and views of those outside the group can be discredited, and hence nothing will disturb the process of polarization as group members continue to talk. Deliberating enclaves of like-minded people are often a breeding ground for extreme movements. Terrorists are made, not born, and terrorist networks often operate in just this way. As a result, they can move otherwise ordinary people to violent acts.[7] But the point goes well beyond such domains. Group polarization occurs in our daily lives; it involves our economic decisions, our evaluations of our neighbors, even our decisions about what to eat, what to drink, and where to live.

To understand the nature of the basic phenomenon and its power and generality, let me outline three studies in which I have personally been involved.

RED STATES, BLUE STATES

In 2005, Reid Hastie, David Schkade, and I conducted a small experiment in democracy in Colorado.[8] About sixty American citizens were brought together and assembled into ten groups, usually consisting of six people. Members of each group were asked to deliberate on three of the most controversial issues of the day.

Should states allow same-sex couples to enter into civil unions?
Should employers engage in "affirmative action" by giving a preference to members of traditionally disadvantaged groups?
Should the United States sign an international treaty to combat global warming?

As the experiment was designed, the groups consisted of "liberal" and "conservative" members—the former from Boulder, the latter from Colorado Springs. It is widely known that Boulder tends to be liberal and that Colorado Springs tends to be conservative. The groups were screened to ensure that their members generally conformed to these stereotypes. For example, group members were asked to report on their assessment of Vice President Dick Cheney. In Boulder, those who liked him were cordially excused from the experiment. In Colorado Springs, those who disliked him were similarly excused.

In this way, the experiment involved groups of like-minded people. In the parlance of election years in the United States, the experiment created five "Blue State" groups and five "Red State" groups—five groups whose members initially tended toward liberal positions in general and five whose members tended toward conservative positions. On the three issues that interested us, however, participants were not screened at all. There was no way of knowing their precise views on civil unions, affirmative action, and climate change. Participants were asked to state their opinions anonymously both before and after fifteen minutes of group discussion, and also to try to reach a public verdict before the final anonymous statement. Their opinions were registered on a scale of 0–10, where 0 meant "disagree very strongly," 5 meant "disagree slightly," and 10 meant "agree very strongly" with the relevant proposition (states should allow civil unions for same-sex couples, employers should maintain affirmative action programs, the United States should sign an international agreement to control global warming). We were especially interested in a single question: How would people's private, anonymous statements of their views change as a result of a brief period of discussion?

As the experiment unfolded, people in both Boulder and Colorado Springs were polite, engaged, and substantive. They treated each other with civility and respect. I have seen the videos of several of these discussions, and it is fair to say that for most of the participants, there was an effort to think hard, to listen to others, and to be reasonable. What was the effect of discussion? There were three critical findings.

More Extremism

In almost every group, members ended up with more extreme positions after they spoke with one another. Most of the liberals in Boulder favored an international treaty to control global warming before discussion; their enthusiasm increased after discussion. Most of the conservatives in Colorado were neutral on that treaty before discussion; they strongly opposed it after discussion. Discussion made same-sex civil unions more popular among the liberals in Boulder; discussion made civil unions less popular among conservatives in Colorado Springs. Mildly favorable toward affirmative action before discussion, liberals became strongly favorable toward affirmative action after discussion. Firmly negative about affirmative action before discussion, conservatives became even more negative about affirmative action after discussion.

Much Less Internal Diversity

The experiment had a separate effect, one that is equally important: It made both liberal groups and conservative groups significantly more homogeneous—and thus squelched diversity. Before members started to talk, many groups displayed a fair bit of internal disagreement. The group disagreements were reduced as a result of a mere fifteen-minute discussion. Note that the primary test here involves what happened to their *anonymous* statements. How diverse were people's predeliberation views, on these issues, compared with their postdeliberation views? In their private statements, group members showed far more consensus after discussion than before.

Greater Rifts

It follows that discussion helped to widen the rift between liberals and conservatives on all three issues. Before discussion, some liberal groups were, on some issues, fairly close to some conservative groups. The result of discussion was to divide them far more sharply.

Here, then, is an initial indication of why groups go to extremes. When people talk to like-minded others, they tend to amplify their preexisting views, and to do so in a way that reduces their internal diversity. We see this happen in politics; it happens in families, businesses, churches and synagogues, and student organizations as well.

FEDERAL JUDGES AND POLARIZED DIFFERENCES

For many decades, the United States has been conducting a truly extraordinary natural experiment involving group behavior, moderation, and extremism. The experiment involves federal judges, who are randomly assigned into groups that look a bit like Boulder and Colorado Springs. What can we learn from this experiment? The simplest lesson is that no less than ordinary citizens, like-minded judges go to extremes. This is a striking finding, because judges are specialists and learned in the law; they are not supposed to be so vulnerable to the political inclinations of their colleagues.

On federal courts of appeals, judicial panels consist of three judges. The possible panel compositions are just four: (a) three Republican appointees, (b) three Democratic appointees, (c) two Republican appointees and one Democratic appointee, and (d) two Democratic appointees and one Republican appointee. Panel assignments are random, and the sample is very large. For this reason, it is possible to test whether judicial votes are affected by panel composition—that is, whether Republican and Democratic appointees vote differently depending on whether they are sitting with Republican or Democratic appointees. Do we observe anything like group polarization among federal judges?

For present purposes, the key questions are these: How do Republican appointees vote on panels consisting solely of Republican appointees (RRR panels)? How do Democratic appointees vote on panels consisting solely of Democratic appointees (DDD panels)? RRR panels are a bit like Colorado Springs, and DDD panels are a bit like Boulder. Do federal judges behave as citizens do in the Colorado experiment? More specifically, we might ask whether Republican appointees, on RRR panels, behave differently from Republican appointees on RRD panels or RDD panels, and whether Democratic appointees, on DDD panels, behave differently from Democratic appointees on DDR or DRR panels. Do like-minded judges show especially distinctive voting patterns?

The phenomenon of group polarization tells us what to expect. Both Democratic and Republican appointees should show extreme behavior on panels that are unified, that is, on DDD and RRR panels. Wherever Democratic appointees and Republican appointees show a general difference in voting patterns, that difference will be *amplified* if we compare Democratic appointees on DDD panels with Republican appointees on RRR panels. To test this claim, we might want to compare two figures: (a) the total difference between the liberal voting rates of Democratic appointees and that of Republican appointees and (b) the difference between the liberal voting rates of Democratic appointees on all-Democratic panels and the liberal voting rates of Republican appointees on all-Republican panels. The latter difference—between Democratic appointees on DDD panels and Republican appointees on RRR panels—might be called the *polarized difference*.

In countless areas, Democratic appointees show especially liberal voting patterns on all-Democratic panels. Republican appointees show especially conservative voting patterns on all-Republican panels. If we aggregate all cases showing an ideological difference between the two groups, we find a 15 percent difference between Republican and Democratic appointees in liberal voting rates. That is a pretty big difference. But the polarized difference is far higher—34 percent!

Our method was quite simple. We collected tens of thousands of judicial votes, mostly in ideologically contested cases, including race discrimination, sex discrimination, disability discrimination, affirmative action, campaign finance, environmental protection, labor, and free speech. We used simple, relatively uncontroversial tests to code decisions as "liberal" or "conservative." For example, a judicial ruling in favor of an African American plaintiff, alleging race discrimination, was coded as liberal. Similarly, we characterized as liberal a vote that fits the usual political stereotypes—to uphold an affirmative action program, a campaign finance restriction, an environmental regulation challenged as too aggressive, or a decision of the National Labor Relations Board in favor of employees. True, these tests of whether a judicial decision is liberal are pretty crude. But because the sample is so big, we are able to discern clear and illuminating patterns; the crudeness of the tests does not seem to have introduced distortions.

Consider just a few key examples.[9]

- In gay rights cases, the overall spread between Republican appointees and Democratic appointees is 41 percent—Republican appointees vote in favor of gay rights 16 percent of the time compared with a 57 percent rate for Democratic appointees. But if we compare how Democratic appointees vote on DDD panels to how Republican appointees vote on RRR panels, the polarized difference turns out to be more than double—86 percent! In our data set, Republican appointees vote pro–gay rights 14 percent of the time on RRR panels—compared with 100 percent for Democratic appointees on DDD panels.

- In cases involving disability discrimination, the overall difference is 18 percent; the polarized difference is nearly double, at 33 percent.
- In cases involving decisions by the Environmental Protection Agency, the overall difference in voting is 15 percent; the polarized difference is no less than 36 percent.
- In affirmative action cases, the overall difference is a significant 28 percent; the polarized difference is a whopping 49 percent.
- In sex discrimination cases, the overall difference is 17 percent; the polarized difference is nearly triple, at 46 percent.

If all of the evidence is taken as a whole, the lesson is unmistakable. It is not exactly shocking to find that Republican and Democratic appointees show significantly different voting patterns. But the overall difference is much smaller than the polarized difference—the difference between how Republican appointees vote when sitting only with Republican appointees and how Democratic appointees vote when sitting only with Democratic appointees. On this score, judges do not look a whole lot different from citizens in Colorado Springs and Boulder. When they sit with like-minded others, they become more extreme.

One qualification: While this is the central pattern in many areas of the law, there are three areas in which judges are not affected by the panel's composition. In those areas, both Republican and Democratic appointees vote the same whether they are in the minority or part of a unified panel. The three areas are abortion, capital punishment, and national security. Apparently judges have such strong convictions in such cases that they are not affected by what their colleagues say or do. I will return to this point later; it offers an important cautionary note about my central claims. Sometimes people feel really strongly, and the views of others do not move them.

PUNISHING WRONGDOERS

Now let us turn to the behavior of juries and, in particular, to the effects of deliberation on punitive damage awards. This is a pretty technical area, but an understanding of those effects will, I hope, illuminate a number of issues including but extending well beyond politics and law.

In American law, punitive damage awards are of major importance in their own right. Companies are greatly concerned about unpredictable and sometimes very high awards, in the hundreds of millions of dollars. Many people have tried to develop ways to discipline jury decisions, and the Supreme Court has taken an active interest in the problem. More important still, punitive damage awards provide an excellent area in which to study the consequences of discussion on group behavior, especially for people who display a degree of outrage—and outrage is one of my central concerns here.

If group members begin with a degree of outrage, do deliberating groups become more outraged or less so? The answer bears on social movements and political protests of many different kinds. As we shall see, it also bears on feuds, ethnic conflict, and even family behavior. When a child is upset at unfair behavior at school, how are parents likely to react? When a husband is angry about unfairness directed at him at work, how will a wife react, and how will his wife's reaction affect him?

To understand the jury experiments, conducted with Daniel Kahneman and David Schkade, we must begin with a study of individuals, not groups, involving about 1,000 people, who were asked to register their judgments about misconduct by a corporate defendant.[10] The goal was to understand why punitive damage awards are so variable: Why do some juries come up with awards of $100,000 and others with awards of $1 million, in cases that seem pretty similar? We asked people to record their judgments on three different scales. The first was a bounded scale of 0 to 6, involving the outrageousness of the company's behavior. Each of the points along the scale was clearly marked, so that 0 meant "not at all outrageous" and 6 meant "exceptionally outrageous." The second was also a bounded scale of 0 to 6, but this scale measured the desired level of punishment; 0 meant "none" and 6 meant "extremely severe" punishment. The third scale was the unbounded one of dollars. Should the company have to pay $10,000? $100,000? $1 million? More?

Our central findings, involving personal injury cases, were straightforward. People agree on how outrageous corporate misconduct is. They also agree on the appropriate severity of punishment on the bounded scale. But the dollar scale creates a lot of trouble and confusion.

To establish these points, we used a simple technique, in which individual responses are pooled to produce "statistical juries," whose verdict is the judgment of the median member. Having done this, we found that small groups of six people, or statistical juries, usually agree about outrageousness and appropriate punishment. Importantly, the agreement cuts across demographic differences. With the magic of the computer, we can create statistical juries of any imaginable kind—all male, all female, all white, all Hispanic, all African American, all rich, all poor, all old, all young, all well educated, all poorly educated. Demography does not matter. All these groups essentially agree with one another!

By contrast, statistical juries show a lot of variability with respect to dollar awards. The dollar judgment of one jury is not a good predictor of the dollar judgments of other juries. But demography is not the source of the variability; it is not as if rich people disagree with poor people, or old people disagree with young people, or men disagree with women. The problem is the dollar scale. The reason for the variability is that whatever their demographic group, people do not have a clear sense of how to translate their punitive intentions, on a bounded scale, onto the scale of dollars. Does a "6" mean a punishment of $50,000, or $100,000, or $1 million, or $10 million, or more? People just don't know. The dollar scale, bounded at the lower end ($0) and essentially un-bounded at the upper end, lacks signposts that give meaning to the various "points" on the scale. For this reason, people who agree that the case is a "4" on a scale of 0–6 may not agree on the appropriate translation of that figure into some monetary equivalent.

The study I have just described involved an effort to pool individual responses; it did not involve group discussion. If we want to understand how juries actually behave, or how outrage develops in the real world, this is a big defect.

Hence we conducted a follow-up experiment, involving about 3,000 jury-eligible citizens and 500 deliberating juries, each with six people. Our goal was to learn how people would be influenced by seeing and discussing the views of others. Here is how the experiment worked. People read about a personal injury case, including the arguments made by both sides. They were also asked to record, in advance of deliberation, an individual "punishment judgment," now on a scale of 0 to 8, where (again) 0 indicated that the defendant should not be punished at all, and 8 indicated that the defendant should be punished extremely severely. After the individual judgments were recorded, jurors were sorted into six-person groups and asked to deliberate to reach a unanimous "punishment verdict." You might predict (as we did) that people would compromise and that the verdicts of juries would be the median of punishment judgments of jurors. But your prediction would be badly wrong.

Instead, the effect of deliberation was to create both a *severity shift* for high-punishment jurors and a *leniency shift* for low-punishment jurors. When the median judgment of individual jurors was 4 or higher on the 8-point scale, the jury's verdict ended up *higher* than that median judgment. Consider, for example, a case involving a man who nearly drowned on a defectively constructed yacht. Jurors tended to be outraged by the idea of a defectively built yacht, and groups were significantly more outraged than their median members. High levels of outrage and severe punitive judgments became higher and more severe as a result of group interactions.

But when the median judgment of individual jurors was below 4, the jury's verdict was typically *below* that median judgment. Consider a case involving a shopper who was injured in a fall when an escalator suddenly stopped. Individual jurors were not greatly bothered by the incident, seeing it as a genuine accident rather than a case of serious wrongdoing. In such cases, juries were more lenient than individual jurors. Here, then, is a lesson about what happens when people discuss wrongdoing. If group members are upset, they will probably get more upset after talking to each other. If group members think that what happened is not a big deal, they will usually think that what happened is basically nothing after a period of discussion.

With dollar awards, by contrast, juries were systematically more severe in their awards than the median juror. Even the small awards were typically higher than the award selected by the median juror before people started to talk. Here is the most striking finding: *In 27 percent of the cases, the jury's award was at least as high as that of the highest predeliberation judgment of the members of that particular jury!* Hence the shift toward more severity, and more extremism, was especially pronounced with dollars. It follows, by the way, that the monetary awards by deliberating juries were even more unpredictable than the monetary awards by statistical juries.

Let me underline our two key findings. The first is that when people begin with a high level of outrage and favor some kind of aggressive responses, groups are more aggressive than individuals. The second is that for monetary awards, juries are significantly more extreme than jurors.

TAKING RISKS

What happens when people who are inclined to take risks talk with other people who are inclined to take risks? The answer is that they become still more inclined to take risks.[11]

Consider, for example, the questions whether to take a new job, to invest in a foreign country, to escape from a prisoner-of-war camp, or to run for political office.[12] With respect to many decisions, members of deliberating groups became significantly more disposed to take risks after a brief period of collective discussion. On the basis of such evidence, it became standard to believe that deliberation produced a systematic "risky shift." For a significant period, the major consequence of group discussion, it was thought, was to produce that risky shift—a thought that would bear on many parts of social life, because groups are often asked to decide whether to take a gamble or, instead, to take precautions.

But later studies drew this conclusion into serious question. They even raised the question whether culture, rather than group dynamics, is responsible for the risky shift. On many of the same questions on which Americans displayed a risky shift, Taiwanese subjects showed a "cautious shift."[13] On most of the topics just listed, deliberation led citizens of Taiwan to become significantly less risk-inclined than they were before they started to talk. Nor was the cautious shift limited to the Taiwanese. Among Americans, deliberation sometimes produced a cautious shift as well, as risk-averse people became more reluctant to take certain risks after they talked with one another.[14] There are two major examples of cautious shifts: the decision whether to marry (!) and the decision whether to board a plane despite severe abdominal pain, possibly requiring medical attention. In these cases, the members of deliberating groups moved toward greater caution.

At first glance, it seemed hard to reconcile these competing findings, but the reconciliation turned out to be simple: *The predeliberation median is the best predictor of the direction of the shift.*[15] When group members are disposed toward risk-taking, a risky shift is observed. When members are disposed toward caution, a cautious shift is observed. It follows that the striking difference between American and Taiwanese subjects is not a product of any cultural difference in how people behave in groups. It results from a difference in the predeliberation medians of the Americans and the Taiwanese on the key questions.[16] When Americans show a predeliberation median in favor of caution, discussion moves them toward greater caution; the same is true of Taiwanese. When American groups show a risky shift, and Taiwanese a cautious shift, it is simply because of a difference in their initial inclinations. Thus the risky shift and the cautious shift are both subsumed under the general rubric of group polarization.

It is tempting to wonder whether group polarization is a product of particular cultures and particular "types." But as

I have noted, there is no nation on earth in which group polarization has been found not to occur. I will return, however, to some ways of counteracting it.

In the behavioral laboratory, group polarization has been shown in a remarkably wide range of contexts.[17] How good-looking are certain people? Group deliberation produces more extreme judgments about that question: If individuals think that someone is good-looking, the group is likely to think that person is devastatingly attractive.[18] (Movie stars undoubtedly benefit from this process.) Group polarization also occurs for obscure factual questions, such as how far Sodom (on the Dead Sea) is below sea level.[19] Even burglars show a shift in the cautious direction when they discuss prospective criminal endeavors.[20] In a revealing finding at the intersection of cognitive and social psychology, groups have been found to make more, rather than fewer, "conjunction errors" (believing that A and B are more likely to be true than A alone) than individuals when individual error rates are high—though fewer when individual error rates are low.[21]

To get a sense of the power of group polarization in the domains of law and politics, consider just a few more studies. After deliberation, groups of people turn out to be far more inclined to protest apparently unfair behavior than was their median member before discussion began.[22] Consider, for example, the appropriate response to three different events: police brutality against African Americans, an apparently unjustified war, and sex discrimination by a local city council. *In every one of these contexts, deliberation made group members far more likely to support aggressive protest action.* Group members moved, for example, from support for a peaceful march to support for a nonviolent demonstration, such as a sit-in at a police station or city hall. Interestingly, the size of the shift toward a more extreme response was correlated with the initial mean. When people initially supported a strong response, group discussion produced a greater shift in the direction of support for a still stronger response. As we shall see, this finding is standard within the literature: The shift toward extremism is often larger when the average person starts with a pretty extreme position.[23]

People often make individual judgments about fairness and unfairness; they also make those judgments in groups. What happens to our judgments about unfairness when we speak with one another? The answer should now be clear: When we are individually inclined to believe that unfairness has occurred, our discussion will intensify our beliefs and make us very angry.[24] The relevant studies were quite realistic. People were asked to engage in tasks designed to simulate activities that might actually be undertaken in a business setting—such as classifying budget items, scheduling meetings, and routing a phone message through the proper channels with assignment of the proper level of priority. Good performance could produce financial rewards. After completing the tasks, people were able to ask for their supervisors' judgments and receive feedback from them. Some of the answers seemed rude and unfair, such as "I've decided not to read your message. The instructions say it's up to me . . . so don't bother sending me any other messages or explanations about your performance on this task" and "If you would have worked harder, then you'd have scored higher. I will not accept your message on this round!"

People were asked to rate their supervisors along various dimensions, including fairness, politeness, bias, and good leadership. The ratings occurred in three periods. The first included individual ratings, the second included a group consensus judgment, and the third included individual ratings after group judgment. It turned out that group judgments were far more negative than the average of individual judgments.[25] In many cases, group members decided that the behavior was really very unfair, even though individuals believed that the behavior was only mildly unfair. Interestingly, the groups' conclusions were typically more extreme than were people's individual judgments after deliberation. But such judgments were nonetheless more negative, and thus more extreme, than predeliberation individual judgments.

These findings are remarkably similar to those involving juror outrage, where, as we have seen, groups are more outraged than their median member. We now have a strong clue about the sources of protest movements, a topic that I explore in due course. For the moment, let us try to explain group polarization.

CHAPTER 2

Extremism
Why and When

In this chapter, my major goal is to answer two questions: Why do like-minded people go to extremes? And when do they do so? As we shall see, the answers to those questions bear on an exceedingly wide range of social puzzles, including the immense power of authorities, the nature of "evil," the idea of groupthink, and social cascades, by which large groups of people move in new directions in terms of their investments, their political choices, and even their religious convictions.

The most important reason for group polarization, and a key to extremism in all its forms, involves the exchange of new information. Group polarization often occurs because people are telling one another what they know, and what they know is skewed in a predictable direction. When they listen to each other, they move.

NEW INFORMATION

Suppose that you are in a group of people whose members tend to think that Israel is the real aggressor in the Mideast conflict, that eating beef is unhealthy, or that same-sex unions are a good idea. In such a group, you will hear many arguments to that effect. Because of the initial distribution of views, you will hear relatively fewer opposing views. It is highly likely that you will have heard some, but not all, of the arguments that emerge from the discussion. After you have heard all of what is said, you will probably shift further in the direction of thinking that Israel is the real aggressor, opposing eating beef, and favoring civil unions. And even if you do not shift—even if you are impervious to what others think—most group members will probably be affected.

When groups move, they do so in large part because of the impact of information.[1] Happily, people tend to respond to the arguments made by other people—and the pool of arguments, in a group with a predisposition in a particular direction, will inevitably be skewed in the direction of the original predisposition.

Certainly this can happen in a group whose members tend to support aggressive government regulation to combat climate change. Group members will hear a number of arguments in favor of aggressive government regulation and fewer arguments the other way. If people are listening, they will have a stronger conviction, in the same direction from which they began, as a result of deliberation. If people are worried about climate change, the arguments they offer will incline them toward greater worry. If people start with the belief that climate change is a hoax and a myth, their discussions will amplify and intensify that belief. And indeed, a form of "environmental tribalism" is an important part of modern political life. Some groups are indifferent to environmental problems that greatly concern and even terrify others. The key reason is the information to which group members are exposed. If you hear that genetically modified food poses serious risks, and if that view is widespread in your community, you might end up frightened. If you hear nothing about the risks associated with genetically modified food, except perhaps that some zealots are frightened, you will probably ridicule their fear. And when groups move in dangerous directions—toward killing and destruction—it is usually because the flow of information supports that movement.

CORROBORATION

Those who lack confidence and who are unsure what they should think tend to moderate their views.[2] Suppose that you are asked what you think about some question on which you lack information. You are likely to avoid extremes. It is for this reason that cautious people, not knowing what to do, tend to choose some midpoint between the extremes.[3] But if other people seem to share their views, people become more confident that they are correct. As a result, they will probably move in a more extreme direction.

In a wide variety of experimental contexts, people's opinions have been shown to become more extreme simply because their initial views have been corroborated and because they have been more confident after learning of the shared views of others.[4] Suppose that other people share your view that the United States is not to be trusted, that the attacks of 9/11 were staged, or that Iran poses a serious threat to the rest of the world. If so, your own view will be more deeply felt after you hear what they have to say. Note that there is an obvious connection between this explanation and the finding that Republican appointees on a panel of three Republican appointees are likely to be more extreme than Republican appointees on a panel with only two such judges. The existence of unanimous confirmation, from two others, will strengthen confidence—and hence strengthen extremity.[5]

What is especially noteworthy is that this process—of increased confidence and increased extremism—is often occurring simultaneously for all participants. Suppose that a group of four people is inclined to distrust the intentions of the United States with respect to foreign aid. Seeing her tentative view confirmed by three others, each member is likely to feel vindicated, to hold her view more confidently, and to move in a more extreme direction. At the same time, the very same internal movements are also occurring in *other* people (from corroboration to more confidence, and from more confidence to more extremism). But those movements will not be highly visible to each participant. It will simply appear as if others "really" hold their views without hesitation. As a result, our little group might conclude, after a day's discussion, that the intentions of the United States, with respect to foreign aid, cannot be trusted at all.

We have a clue here about the great importance of social networks, on the Internet and in ordinary life, in creating movements of various sorts. Social networks can operate as polarization machines because they help to confirm and thus amplify people's antecedent views. Those who are inclined to support a cause or a candidate may become quite excited if support is widespread on their social network. In 2008, President Barack Obama greatly benefited from this process, in a way that created extreme enthusiasm for his candidacy. Some of this was planned; his campaign self-consciously promoted social networks that spread favorable information.

But some of this was spontaneous. Obama supporters, especially young people, worked hard on their own to take advantage of existing networks and create new ones that would turn curiosity and tentative support into intense enthusiasm and active involvement.

A very different example is provided by Islamic terrorism, which is also fueled by spontaneous social networks, in which like-minded people discuss grievances with potentially violent results.[6] Terrorism specialist Marc Sageman explains that at certain stages, "the interactivity among a 'bunch of guys' acted as an echo chamber, which progressively radicalized them collectively to the point where they were ready to collectively join a terrorist organization. Now the same process is taking place online."[7] The major force here is not Web sites, which people read passively; it consists of Listservs, blogs, and discussion forums, "which are crucial in the process of radicalization."[8] As we shall see in more detail, Islamic terrorism is a product, in significant part, of group polarization.

These are examples from the political domain, but there are plenty of other illustrations. Why are some cars popular in some areas, but not at all popular in others? Why are some foods enjoyed, or thought to be especially healthy, in some places, whereas the same foods are disliked, or thought to be unhealthy, in other places? Joseph Heinrich and his coauthors note that "[m]any Germans believe that drinking water after eating cherries is deadly; they also believe that putting ice in soft drinks is unhealthy. The English, however, rather enjoy a cold drink of water after some cherries; and Americans love icy refreshments."[9] Why is the same music liked, or hated, among groups of teenagers? Here, too, corroboration greatly matters.

A less innocuous example: In some nations, strong majorities believe that Arab terrorists were not responsible for the attacks of September 11, 2001. According to the Pew Research Institute, 93 percent of Americans believe that Arab terrorists destroyed the World Trade Center, whereas only 11 percent of Kuwaitis believe that Arab terrorists destroyed the World Trade Center.[10] With respect to daily life, a great deal of what we believe, like, and dislike is influenced by the exchange of information and by corroboration.

REPUTATION

A few years ago, I was discussing group polarization with a philosopher who works on the topic of animal rights and animal welfare. He is strongly committed to reducing the suffering of animals, and he told me the following story: "On Friday of a three-day conference, we are perfectly sensible, by my lights. But by Sunday, we stop thinking straight! We become much too extreme. By Sunday, people start saying that no experiment on animals ever produced useful knowledge for human beings. By Sunday, people start saying that it is never acceptable to eat meat, even if animals lived a very long and very happy life, and died of natural causes. Some of us have, in a way, lost our minds." The philosopher told me that this change in view—a form of polarization—was not adequately explained by the exchange of new information or by increased confidence.

What he had in mind was a third explanation, involving social comparison. That explanation begins with the claim that people want to be perceived favorably by other group members, and also to perceive themselves favorably. Sometimes our views are, to a greater or lesser extent, a function of how we want to present ourselves. Of course, some people are more concerned than others with their self-presentation. But once we hear what others believe, some of us will adjust our positions at least slightly in the direction of the dominant position, to hold onto our preserved self-presentation. We might contain our opposition; we might voice somewhat more enthusiasm for the majority view than we really feel.

Some people might want to show, for example, that they are not timid or cautious, especially in an entrepreneurial group that disparages these characteristics and favors boldness and risk-taking. In business, people often want to seem to be risk takers. In such a group, people will frame their position so that they do not appear timid or cautious by comparison with other group members. And when they hear what other people think, they might find that they occupy a somewhat different position, in relation to the group, from what they hoped. They will shift accordingly.[11] This might be because they want others to see them in a certain way. Or it might be because they want to see themselves a certain way, and a shift is necessary so that they can see themselves in the most attractive light.

Suppose, for example, that group members believe that they are somewhat more opposed to capital punishment than are most people. Such people might shift a bit after finding themselves in a group of people who are strongly opposed to capital punishment, simply to maintain their preferred self-presentation. Does the example seem unrealistic? Consider the otherwise inexplicably extreme behavior of many Republicans and many Democrats in the debate over the Bush Gore presidential vote in Florida in 2000. Reasonable people could differ at the time. Each side had something to say. But many members of both parties, talking and listening mostly to one another, suggested that the other party was trying to "steal the election." This is one example of what happens in nearly all presidential elections. In 2008, for example, many supporters of Senator John McCain ended up in unfounded and indefensible positions, urging and apparently thinking that President Obama "palled around with terrorists" and might even be disloyal to the country. The phenomenon occurs in many contexts. People might wish not to seem too enthusiastic about, or too restrained in their enthusiasm for, affirmative action, feminism, or an increase in national defense; hence their views shift when they see what other group members think. The result is to press the group's position toward one or another extreme, and also to induce shifts in individual members.

To understand the importance of social comparison, consider the important finding that low-status members of groups become ever more reluctant, over the course of discussion, to repeat privately held information,[12] that is, information that they hold but that others do not. Those in the group who are inexperienced, or are thought to be low on the hierarchy, are particularly loath to emphasize their privately held information as discussion proceeds. Suppose that the leaders of a religious organization are suspected of wrongdoing. How many people, low on the totem pole, will hold them to account?

The empirical findings suggest that group members, and especially lower status ones, are nervous about emphasizing information that most group members lack. Indeed, lower status members will often drop uniquely held information very rapidly—partly because of the difficulty of establishing its credibility and relevance, and partly because they risk the group's disapproval if they press a line of argument that others reject. In many deliberating groups, people who emphasize uniquely held information take an obvious social risk, and they know it. Note in this regard that group members typically *underestimate* the performance of low-status members and typically *overestimate* the performance of high-status members, in a way that gives high-status members a degree of deference that is not warranted by reality.[13]

In the same vein, those who discuss shared information obtain rewards in the form of an enhanced sense of competence in the eyes of others—and in their own eyes as well.[14] Important but perhaps obvious: If someone tells you something you already know, you are likely to like that person a little bit better as a result. Important and less obvious: If someone tells you something you already know, you are likely to like *yourself* a bit better as a result! In face-to-face discussions and in purely written tasks, people give higher ratings (in terms of knowledge, competence, and credibility) both to themselves and to others after receiving information that they knew already. The general problem is that deliberating groups often move to unjustified extremes because they fail to elicit information that could steer them in the right directions.

A political example: In the presidency of George W. Bush, many failures occurred because of an unfortunate culture that encouraged, rather than combated, group polarization.[15] In the words of Scott McClellan,

> Bush's way of managing the problems in Iraq was proving inadequate to the task ... [H]e was insulated from the reality of events on the ground and consequently began falling into the trap of believing his own spin. He failed to spend enough time seeking independent input from a broad range of outside experts, those beyond the White House bubble who had first-hand experience on the ground in Iraq, and—perhaps most important—those with differing points of view, including those who disagreed with his position.[16]

By contrast, Lincoln's presidency has been described as a healthy Team of Rivals,[17] in which Lincoln self-consciously chose diverse people who could challenge his inclinations and test one another's arguments in the interest of producing the most sensible judgments. Unfortunately and even tragically, the Bush administration turned into a Team of Unrivals, in which internal diversity and dissent were squelched as disloyal. With respect to the Iraq war, tax policy, regulation, and spending, group polarization operated in full force, and the administration's leaders took no steps to combat it. Reputational pressures, of a particularly acute form, ensured extremism, confidence, and uniformity.

Genocide offers an especially grim example of this phenomenon. How can apparently ordinary people turn into killers? Information plays a major role. When people are informed that killing is right or even necessary, they might be willing to kill. In the words of a participant in the genocide in Rwanda: "When you have been prepared the right way by the radios and the official advice, you obey more easily, even if the order is to kill your neighbors."[18] But as another killer suggested, reputational pressures produce killing as well: "If you proved too green with the machete, you could find yourself deprived of rewards, to nudge you in the right direction. If you got laughed at one day, you did not take long to shape up. If you went home empty-handed, you might even be scolded by your wife or your children."[19]

TWO FUNCTIONS OF POLARIZATION

We should distinguish between two different accounts of group polarization. One account suggests that polarization reveals hidden beliefs and desires. A very different account insists that polarization creates new beliefs and desires.

On the first account, people often have a suppressed but deep-seated set of concerns. These concerns do not ordinarily materialize in social life; they usually remain unspoken.

The concerns are not unthought, but they are, in extreme cases, unthinkable, in the sense that they really cannot be voiced in public without creating serious risks of social disapproval or even ostracism.[20] Now imagine that group members speak with one another, and those suppressed concerns come to the surface. As people exchange tales and reactions, the unthinkable comes out into the open. One result is more extremism, as people feel outrage about practices that used to produce self-silencing.[21] Consider the context of disability, where this is a plausible account. Among disabled people, the objections to the status quo are there, but they are sometimes buried, and discussion brings them out.

Compare the issue of sex equality. The whole idea of consciousness-raising is designed to signal the existence of repressed angers and objections; once people speak with one another, consciousness is raised in the sense that those angers and objections come to the surface. What was once suppressed, perhaps on the ground that powerful people would object, is now voiced; people articulate their concerns as a result of group discussions. What was once unthinkable is now in the public domain. On this view, deliberation can create a kind of self-discovery, in which the authentic inner voice becomes articulate.[22] Here deliberation *reveals* something that unquestionably existed before.

The area of sexual harassment is a particularly revealing example. Women did not exactly like being harassed, but before the practice was unlawful, or even had a name, their anger was muted. Once women spoke to one another in an open way, and in the midst of the emerging women's movement, a silenced group was ready to speak out. Attacking sexual harassment was once, in a sense, unthinkable. Even the phrase did not exist. In many places, defending sexual harassment is now unthinkable (even if

significant numbers of men may not believe that it is quite
so bad).

On the competing account, group polarization can occur
even if there is no initial sense of grievance; little or perhaps
nothing was suppressed. Instead social influences, involving
the efforts of *polarization entrepreneurs*, give rise to intensifying objections and growing protest. For many group members, the views that end up being extreme are entirely
generated by group interactions. People may not have a
deep-seated belief that climate change is occurring or that
some apparent opponent is bad or corrupt or badly motivated. But as they speak with one another, their inclination
to accept that belief is intensified. Here deliberation creates,
for some or many, a series of objections that had previously
been absent.

We can imagine this phenomenon in the political
domain, as people develop an initial concern with some
practice or person, and that initial concern intensifies as a
result of internal discussions. For some disabled people and
some women, this competing account undoubtedly captures reality. In the important domain of ethnic identification, we will encounter some important examples.
Religious beliefs and practices often arise and intensify in
exactly this way.

From the point of view of those who are subject to it,
group polarization is often entirely rational. You are in a
group of people, discussing climate change or same-sex
marriage. You hear a set of arguments. Your initial inclinations are confirmed. You like the other group members,
and you want them to like you. In these circumstances,
increased extremism, on your part, may be a perfectly
rational reaction to what you learn and to what you care
about. This sunny picture of polarization—from the standpoint of those who fall prey to it—undoubtedly captures

much of reality.[23] When people shift in groups, it is often for perfectly sensible reasons. The point applies broadly and in some settings where sense isn't exactly the currency of the realm; it suggests that political extremists and conspiracy theorists may well be responding rationally to what they hear and learn.[24]

But there are two major wrinkles. The first is that to the extent that people are motivated by a concern for their reputation, they might not be moving because of information and good arguments. If people who believe in animal rights are shifting not because of what they hear, but because of how they want to seem, their shift might make little sense on the merits. The second and subtler wrinkle is that much of the time, people do not seem to have anything like an adequate sense of the partiality and skew of the groups in which they find themselves. If you are in a group of people who lean to the left or to the right, you should adjust your reactions to what they say, simply because of the inclinations of those in the group. If people in your own company are especially optimistic about a certain course of action and dismissive about the plans of a competitor, you might want to take into account the likely biases that surround you. If those who surround the president or the governor seem to think that a certain economic plan is terrific, the president or the governor ought to consider the possibility that the group's members start out in favor of the plan, and are hardly a representative sample of expert opinion.

I suspect, in fact, that group polarization often occurs because of people's failure to adjust their reactions to the skewed compositions of the groups in which they find themselves.[25] We act as if those groups reflect an impartial sum of information, even when there is a systematic bias. This tendency can get us into a lot of trouble in many areas, warping our judgments not only about politics but also about health, money, and religion. Indeed, financial crises often stem from processes of this kind, as groups with their own biases create speculative bubbles in (say) real estate and Internet stocks—and then produce panics.

Recall the importance of distinguishing between two different kinds of polarization: planned and spontaneous. As we have seen, some people act as polarization entrepreneurs: They attempt to create communities of like-minded people, and they are aware that these communities will not only harden positions but also move them to a more extreme point. But sometimes polarization arises spontaneously, through entirely voluntary choices, without the slightest kind of planning. Consider, for example, people's reading patterns, which suggest an unmistakable form of self-sorting into liberal and conservative networks.[26] Or consider the blogosphere itself, which shows a similar kind of spontaneous sorting and polarization.[27] Or consider simple geographical choices; like-minded people, in essential agreement on political issues, may end up living in the same area simply because that is what they want to do.[28] We shall encounter many examples of both planned and spontaneous polarization.

"RHETORICAL ADVANTAGE" AND SKEWED DEBATES

A Mysterious Finding

In the context of punitive damage awards by juries, a particular finding deserves special attention. Recall that jurors were asked to record their dollar judgments in advance of deliberation and then to deliberate together to produce dollar verdicts. The principal effect was to make nearly *all* awards go up, in the sense that the jury's dollar award typically exceeded the median award of individual jurors.[29] There is a further point. The effect of deliberation in increasing dollar awards was most pronounced in the case of high awards. For example, the median *individual* judgment, in the case involving the defective yacht, was $450,000, whereas the median *jury* judgment, in that same case, was $1 million. But awards shifted upward for low awards as well.

Here is the mystery: Why did all awards go up? Why didn't the low ones, at least, go down? A tempting explanation, consistent with group polarization, is that any positive median award suggests a predeliberation tendency to punish—and as usual, deliberation aggravates that tendency by increasing awards. But even if this explanation is correct, it does not seem nearly specific enough. The striking fact is that those arguing for higher awards seem to have an automatic *rhetorical advantage* over those arguing for lower awards. The intriguing possibility is that in many domains, one point of view has such a rhetorical advantage over other points of view, with predictable results for both thought and behavior.

Daniel Kahneman, David Schkade, and I conducted a subsequent study that supported our speculation, at least for punitive damage awards. We asked a large group of University of Chicago law students to participate in an odd little experiment. We told them that they were to assume that they were sitting on a jury that was deadlocked on the question of appropriate punishment, with some people supporting a greater award and others supporting a lower award. We asked half of the students to devise arguments that would support a higher award *assuming that they knew nothing about the particular case*. Believe it or not, the law students produced a number of such arguments. For example, they stressed the need to deter this particular wrongdoer, the need to deter other potential wrongdoers, and the importance of ensuring that an injured party received more money.

We asked the other half of the students to devise arguments that would support a lower award—again assuming that they knew nothing about the particular case. Here, too, the law students produced a number of such arguments. They stressed the risk that a large award would stop companies from engaging in beneficial activity, the danger that a big award might go mostly to lawyers, and the fact that the injured person should not get a windfall benefit. Then we asked both groups whether it was easier to argue for a higher award or a lower one.

The answer was clear: Most people find it easier, just in the abstract, to defend higher punitive awards against corporations than to defend lower awards.[30] Those defending the higher awards have an automatic rhetorical advantage. Even when people know absolutely nothing about the facts of individual cases, they are able to generate appealing arguments in favor of higher awards. It is much harder to produce plausible-sounding arguments in favor of lower awards. Those seeking higher penalties have a built-in advantage.

Doctors, Altruists, and Others

Rhetorical advantages have been found in seemingly distant areas. Suppose that a group of doctors is deciding what steps to take to resuscitate apparently doomed patients. Are individual doctors less likely, or more likely, to support heroic efforts than teams of doctors?

The evidence suggests that as individuals, doctors are less likely to support heroic efforts than teams. The apparent reason is that in cases of conflict, those who favor such efforts have a rhetorical advantage over those who do not.[31] Doctors do not want to seem, to one another, to be willing to give up on a patient and condemn him to death, even when the chance of success is low. For many doctors operating in groups, giving up suggests an indifference to the sanctity of human life, a lack of a strong commitment, perhaps even a lack of confidence in one's own competence. Hence teams of doctors are willing to do more to save people than are individual doctors. In a sense, medical teams turn out to be more extreme. (Patients and family members, take note.)

Individuals behave very differently from teams in the Dictator Game, an experiment used by social scientists to study selfishness and altruism.[32] In this game, a subject is told that she can allocate a sum of money, say $10, between herself and some stranger. What will the subject do? The standard economic prediction is that most subjects will keep all or almost all of the money for themselves; why should we share money with complete strangers? But the standard prediction turns out to be wrong. Most people choose to keep somewhere between $6 and $8 and to share the rest.[33] My question here, however, is not individual behavior but how behavior in the Dictator Game is affected if people are placed in teams—if people decide in groups rather than as individuals. Are groups more altruistic than individuals? The answer is that team members choose still more equal divisions.[34] Once placed in groups, people show a significant shift toward greater generosity.

Why is this? A good answer points to a rhetorical advantage, one that disfavors selfishness even within a group that stands to benefit from it. If you are on a team of people deciding how selfish to be, you might well be less selfish than you would be on your own—just because you do not want to appear to be particularly selfish. Imagine, for example, that you are deliberating with a group of people about how much money to give to charity. Chances are good that the group will end up being more charitable than the median individual, simply because people do not want to appear to be greedy. People's concern for their reputation plays a large role. People's self-conception also matters: Who wants to feel like a greedy person?

Of course, the outcomes here would change if the team in the Dictator Game had some reason to be hostile to those who would benefit from their generosity. We can easily imagine a variation of the Dictator Game in which, for example, people of a relatively poor religious group are deciding how much to allocate to another religious group that is thought to be both hostile and far wealthier. In this variation, the rhetorical advantage would favor greater selfishness.

Rhetorical Advantage Why? Rhetorical Advantage When?

All this leaves some important questions unanswered: What produces a rhetorical advantage? When will we see one? How can we know in what direction the advantage will go?

The simplest answer points to the particular norms that prevail within the group, and norms, of course, vary across time and place. Among most Americans, current norms make it easy to argue for high penalties against corporations for serious misconduct. But we can easily imagine subcommunities within America (corporate headquarters?) in which the rhetorical advantage runs exactly the other way. In such groups, the level of punishment might be expected to decrease, not to increase, as a result of social interactions. And of course, social norms and reputational influences are closely entangled. Given existing norms, most juries know that they are likely to seem odd if they want to impose little punishment for really bad corporate misconduct.

In any case, it is easy to envisage many other contexts in which one or another side has an automatic rhetorical advantage. Consider debates over penalties for drug dealers and over changing tax rates. In contemporary American political debates, those favoring higher penalties and lower taxes have a strong upper hand. If one group is arguing for maintaining the current tax rates and another for increasing them, the second will have a real uphill battle. And if some people are arguing for lower penalties for criminal offenses, they had better have some unusually strong arguments. Or imagine discussion within a firm about whether to run a risk, or within a family about whether to take some precautions against a threat that family members face from, say, crime in the neighborhood, a bad economy, or a car that isn't particularly safe. Such a firm might well end up taking the risk, just because those who favor taking the risk have a rhetorical advantage, and for the same reason, such a family might be inclined to take precautions.

Of course, there are limits on the effects of rhetorical advantages. No reasonable person wants taxes to disappear or to impose life sentences for minor drug crimes. But when a rhetorical advantage is involved, group deliberation will produce significant changes in individual judgments. Undoubtedly legislative behavior—involving national security, tax policy, and criminal punishment—is affected by rhetorical advantages. Many movements within judicial panels can be explained in similar terms. True, the governing norms vary from one nation to another. In the United Kingdom and Germany, for example, it is much easier to argue for tax increases than in the United States, especially on polluting behavior; no strong rhetorical advantage is enjoyed by those opposing taxes. In some parts of the world, those resisting restrictions on abortion have a rhetorical advantage; in other parts of the world, they are at a severe disadvantage.

Are rhetorical advantages unhelpful or damaging? In the abstract, this question cannot be answered sensibly. Shifts, including extreme movements, must be evaluated on their merits. Perhaps the higher punitive awards that follow deliberation are simply better. So, too, perhaps, are the movements by doctors toward taking more heroic measures, and by groups deciding to divide funds more equally. The only point is that such advantages exist and that they help to explain social movements, including extreme ones. It would be a surprising stroke of luck if such movements were always benign. When groups become violent, for example, it is often because a rhetorical advantage favors those who press toward more severe responses to real or imagined grievances.

MORE EXTREMISM, LESS EXTREMISM

Group polarization is not a social constant. It can be increased or decreased, and even eliminated, by certain features of group members or their situation.

Extremists Move Most

Recall that in the study of protests, people who started out at a more extreme point showed the greatest shift as a result of group discussion. The point is quite general: Extremists are especially prone to polarization. When people start out at an extreme point and are placed in a group of like-minded people, they are likely to go especially far in the direction toward which they started.[35] There is a lesson here about the sources of terrorism and political violence in general. And because there is a link between confidence and extremism, the confidence of particular members also plays an important role; confident people are more prone to polarization.[36]

Recall that people moderate their opinions if they are unsure whether they are right. And other things being equal, confident people have an advantage in social deliberations. It follows that if group members tend toward extremism, and if the group is dominated by confident people, it is exceedingly likely to shift. In a brilliant essay, Russell Hardin writes that extremists suffer from a *crippled epistemology*.[37] He argues that extremists are often far from irrational. The problem is that they know very little, and what they know supports their extremism. No one doubts that some extremists know a great deal; sometimes extremism is defensible or even right. (The American revolutionaries were extremists; so were Martin Luther King Jr. and Nelson Mandela.) But when groups make unjustified extreme movements—in the direction, for example, of terrorism or genocide—a crippled epistemology is often the reason. Those who start out in an extreme position will be all the more subject to the influences discussed here.

The general point—that extremists are especially prone to significant further shifts—is not limited to the most obvious extremists. The point certainly applies in the business world. Members of a corporate board, inclined to take unusual risks, fall in the same category; the Enron disaster occurred in part as a result of group polarization. The same processes occur within members of a student organization committed, say, to gay rights or to reducing a university's investments in Sudan. So, too, for a government that is determined to avoid, or to make, war. I have suggested that the deliberations of the American government under George W. Bush, culminating in the Iraq war, are a clear example.[38] Tragically, the relatively extreme movement toward war was fueled by antecedent extremism and by an absence of dissenting voices, produced by intense pressure on those who would reject the party line.

Solidarity and Affective Ties Increase Polarization

If members of the group think that they have a shared identity and a high degree of solidarity, there will be heightened polarization.[39] One reason is that if people feel united by some factor (family, politics, or religious convictions), dissent will be dampened. If individual members tend to perceive the others as friendly, likable, and similar to them, the size and likelihood of the shift will increase.[40] The existence of such ties reduces the number of diverse arguments and also intensifies social influences on choice. A clear implication is that mistakes are likely to increase when group members are united mostly through bonds of affection and not through concentration on a particular task; alternative views are least likely to find expression.

By contrast, people are less likely to shift if the direction advocated is being pushed by unfriendly group members or by members who are in some sense "different." A sense of "group belongingness" affects the extent of polarization. In the same vein, physical spacing tends to reduce polarization; a sense of common fate and intragroup similarity tend to increase it, as does the introduction of a rival outgroup.

An interesting experiment investigated the effects of group identification on polarization.[41] Some people were given instructions in which their group membership was made salient (the "group immersion" condition), whereas others were given no such instructions (the "individual" condition). For example, those in the group immersion condition were told that their group consisted solely of first-year psychology students and that they were being tested as group members rather than as individuals. The relevant issues involved affirmative action, government subsidies for the theater, privatization of nationalized industries, and phasing out of nuclear power plants. The results were stunning. Polarization generally occurred, but it was significantly greater when group identity was emphasized. This experiment shows that polarization is highly likely to occur, and to be most extreme, when group membership is made salient.

Compare a related experiment designed to see how group polarization might be dampened.[42] The experiment involved the creation of four-person groups. The experimenters began with tests to establish that all of the groups included equal numbers of persons on two sides of political issues— whether smoking should be banned in public places, whether sex discrimination is a thing of the past, and whether censorship of material for adults infringes on human liberties. People's judgments were registered on a scale running from +4 (strong agreement) to 0 (neutral) to −4 (strong disagreement). In half of the cases (the "uncategorized condition"), people were not made aware that the group consisted of equally divided subgroups. In the other half (the "categorized condition"), people were told that they would find a sharp division in their group, which had equally divided subgroups. They were also informed who was in which group and told that they should sit around the table so that one subgroup was on one side facing the other subgroup.

In the uncategorized condition, discussion generally led to a dramatic reduction in the gap between the two sides. The result was a convergence of opinion toward the middle of the two opposing positions. But things were very different in the categorized condition. Here the shift toward the median was much less pronounced, and frequently there was barely any shift at all. In short, *calling attention to group membership made people far less likely to shift in directions urged by people from different groups.* This little experiment offers a large lesson: If people are told that they are defined by their membership in a certain group— Catholics, Jews, Irish, Russians, Democrats, conservatives—they will be less likely to listen carefully to those who are defined in different terms.

Exit

Over time, group polarization can be fortified by "exit," as moderate members leave the group because they dislike the direction in which things are heading. In a leading study of Islamic terrorism, Marc Sageman emphasizes the importance of this fact. As group members move toward the possibility of violence, there is a situation of voluntary sorting and self-selection in which "only the true believers remain." Those believers regard themselves as "best friends and a substitute for family."[43] These are the most dangerous conditions of all: The groups include extremists, unified by bonds of affection and solidarity, and prone to discussions only among themselves.

The more general point is that when people are prone to exit, the group is likely to become more extreme. The group will end up smaller; its members will be both more like-minded and more willing to take extreme measures. In a kind of vicious circle, that very fact will mean that internal discussions will produce still more extremism. The shifts of student groups in the United States in the 1960s—from relatively moderate forms of left-wing thought to real radicalism and even violence—can be explained partly in these terms. And indeed, this account fits some of the dynamics of the White House under President George W. Bush, as moderate and dissenting officials left the government, leading to the Team of Unrivals that I have mentioned.

It follows that in an important sense, a group is more likely to show extreme movement if it makes it easy for people to leave. If only loyalists stay, the group's median member will be more extreme, and deliberation will produce increasingly extreme movements. Making exit difficult prevents the group from shrinking. But it also ensures that the group will include people who favor relative moderation and tend to discipline its movement toward extremes.

There is a clear connection between these points and Albert Hirschman's important analysis of "exit" and "voice" as responses to disagreement with groups and organizations.[44] Hirschman shows that when exit is freely available, people might simply leave and not use their voices to ensure improved performance. He offers the example of competition between public schools and private schools. If public schools deteriorate, people might exit in favor of private schools. This result will impose some pressure toward improving the public schools, but it will also cause the more significant "loss to the public schools of those member-customers who would be most motivated and determined to put up a fight against the deterioration if they did not have the alternative of the private schools."[45]

What is true for schools is also true for groups that are inclined to go to extremes. An easy exit option will reduce the number of dissenting voices and thus produce greater radicalism. At the same time, the difficulty of exit, combined with strong social pressures, might also reduce dissent, especially because members are likely to be highly dependent on the good will of group members.

Informed Members and Facts

When one or more people in a group are confident that they know the right answer to a factual question, the group might well shift in the direction of accuracy.[46] For such problems, sometimes described as "eureka problems," groups do well; they do not polarize. It is for this reason that groups tend to perform impressively on crossword puzzles. On puzzles, members hardly go to extremes. They accept the correct answer once it is announced. If there is immediate recognition of the correct answer, then groups will arrive at it. With eureka problems, for which the answer, once revealed, is clear to all, deliberation appears to produce accuracy rather than extremism.

Suppose, for example, that the question is how many people were on the earth in 1940, or the number of home runs hit by Barry Bonds, or the distance between Paris and London. Suppose, too, that one or a few people know the right answer. If so, there is a good chance that the group will not polarize, but instead converge on that answer. When this is so, the reason is simple: The person who is confident that she knows the answer will speak with assurance and authority, and she is likely to be convincing for that very reason. If one member of a group is certain that Barry Bonds hit 766 home runs, and if other members are uncertain, then the group might well end up agreeing that he hit 766 home runs.

Of course, it is not inevitable that the result will be agreement on the truth. Social pressures can lead people to blunder even on the simplest factual issues. An impressive study demonstrates that majority pressures can be powerful even for factual questions on which some people know the right answer.[47] The study involved 1,200 people, forming groups of four, five, six members. Individuals were asked true-false questions involving art, poetry, public opinion, geography, economics, and politics. They were then asked to assemble into groups, which discussed the questions and produced answers. The majority played a large role in determining the group's answers. The truth played a role, too, but a lesser one. If a majority of individuals in the group gave the right answer, the group decision moved toward the majority in 79 percent of the cases. If a majority of individuals in the group gave the wrong answer, the group decision nonetheless moved toward the majority in 56 percent of the cases.

Hence the truth did have an influence—79 percent is higher than 56 percent—but the majority's judgment was the dominant influence. And because the majority was influential even when wrong, the average group decision was right only slightly more often than the average individual decision (66 percent vs. 62 percent).

This study demonstrates that groups might err even when some of their members know the truth. In some cases, however, group members who are ignorant will be tentative, and members who are informed will speak confidently. This is enough to promote convergence on truth rather than polarization.

Equally Opposed Subgroups

Return to our study of political beliefs in Boulder and Colorado Springs. What would have happened if we had mixed people from the two places? A tempting response would be that the answer lies in the predeliberation median. If the group's median member favored same-sex unions, perhaps most people would shift in that direction, even if people from Boulder were mixed with those from Colorado Springs.

This might well have happened, but we cannot be sure. The reason is that polarization may not be found when the relevant group consists of individuals drawn equally from two extremes.[48] Suppose that people who initially favor caution are put together with people who initially favor risk-taking. If so, the group judgment may well move toward the middle. Consider a study[49] of six-member groups specifically designed to contain two subgroups (of three persons each) initially committed to opposed extremes; the effect of discussion was to produce movement toward the center. One reason is the existence of relevant information in both directions.

Not surprisingly, this study of equally opposed subgroups found the greatest "depolarization" with obscure matters of fact that carried no emotional resonance—for example, the population of the United States in 1900. It found the least depolarization with highly visible public questions—for example, whether capital punishment is justified. In cases of that kind, people simply stuck with what they thought before. Matters of personal taste depolarized a moderate amount—for example, preference for basketball or football, or for colors to paint a room. It follows that long-debated issues are not likely to depolarize. With respect to such issues, people are simply less likely to shift at all, in part because the arguments are familiar to everyone, and nothing new will emerge from discussion.

We can now offer four conclusions about what might happen within mixed groups.

1. For many issues and many groups, the median point of view, in advance of deliberation, is the best predictor of the direction of the shift; this was indeed what we observed in our study of punitive damage awards by juries.

2. When groups contain equally opposed subgroups, do not hold rigidly to their positions, and listen to one another, members will shift toward the middle; they will depolarize. The effect of mixing will be to produce moderation.

3. When people are dealing with "eureka problems," for which the right answer, once announced, is clear to most or all, mixed groups will find the right answer.
4. Sometimes people will stay exactly where they are. Those with entrenched views on capital punishment, the conflict in the Middle East, or abortion may not be much moved to hear what their adversaries have to say.

These capsule summaries help to explain when one or another of these outcomes is most likely. Standard polarization will occur if there is a well-defined predeliberation tendency in one direction and if people have sufficient open-mindedness that they are likely to listen to one another. Depolarization will occur if group members are split fairly evenly and if people are willing to listen. People will converge on truth if they know it when someone announces it. No movement will occur if people know what they think and think that those who disagree are knaves or fools.

In this regard, return to our studies of judicial behavior. On almost every issue, we observe the pattern I have described, in which Democratic and Republican appointees differ and in which that difference is significantly heightened on all-Democratic and all-Republican panels. But as we have seen, that pattern is not always observed. On three issues, the two sets of appointees do differ, but they do not polarize. Their voting patterns remain the same regardless of whether they are sitting with zero, one, or two people from their own party. In advance, what would you have guessed that the three issues were?

Recall the answer: abortion, capital punishment, and national security. In those domains, Democratic and Republican appointees are simply unable to influence one another. There is a large lesson here for domains in which people's beliefs, preferences, and values are so fixed that social influences are powerless to affect them. And indeed, there is one court of appeals (of twelve) in which Republican and Democratic appointees are generally uninfluenced by one another and in which both sets of appointees do not show more extreme voting patterns on unified panels. I am speaking of the U.S. Court of Appeals for the Sixth Circuit, on which—according to informal lore—Democratic and Republican appointees really don't like each other. Our statistical analysis tends to support the informal lore.

Biased Assimilation

Another set of empirical findings bear directly on the nature and limits of polarization. Suppose that you produced a group of people, half of whom favor capital punishment, and half of whom reject it. Suppose that you gave to the entire group a set of balanced, substantive readings, offering arguments in both directions. What result would you predict? Many people think that we would observe more moderation and hence depolarization. Having seen sensible arguments on the other side, both groups might move to uncertainty, and in that sense to the center.

Surprisingly, this is not what is usually observed.[50] After reading balanced materials offering arguments both ways, opponents of capital punishment are strengthened in their opposition; they become more extreme. Advocates of capital punishment also harden. At least on some issues, people show "biased assimilation."[51] Reading a set of arguments, they discount uncongenial points as silly or stupid and find congenial ones to be smart and pertinent. Hence they are strengthened in their original convictions.

The finding of biased assimilation has important implications for many issues in politics and elsewhere. People often ignore powerful contrary evidence. Some radical movements prosper even when their members are surrounded by information that seems flatly inconsistent with their beliefs. That information can be, and is, discounted as mere propaganda; indeed, its very existence is taken to support people's radical beliefs. Closer to home, our affections, our fears, our judgments, and our preferences often stay fixed, and we retain confidence in them, even when we know enough to shift. Extremists are strongly committed to their beliefs, and when they see evidence that cuts the other way, or even evidence that seems balanced, they can become still more committed, not less so.

So while we have hoped that mixed groups, confronted with balanced information, would polarize less, the opposite is sometimes true. Suppose that the group contains five people who greatly fear climate change and five people who believe that the risks are small. After talking together, and after hearing balanced information, all ten might actually have a stronger commitment to what they thought before they started to talk—and the two groups would be further apart, not less so. I will return shortly to the circumstances in which this unhappy outcome will occur.

Here is an especially disturbing finding. When people's false beliefs are corrected, they might become even firmer in their commitment to those beliefs![52] Suppose, for example, that supporters of the Iraq war were told, by an apparently credible news source and at an early stage, that Iraq did not, in fact, have weapons of mass destruction. Remarkably, such corrections often do not reduce misperceptions, and sometimes they actually increase and strengthen them.

Return here to the problem of terrorism and note the suggestion that intense group dynamics, spawning what Marc Sageman calls a process of "in-group love," ensure that "the group acts as an interactive 'echo chamber,' encouraging escalation of grievances and beliefs in conspiracy to the point of hatred."[53] Group members come to rely exclusively on one another to validate new information, and everything that they believe is a product of interactions within their enclaves. Thus "they discard information refuting their beliefs as propaganda from the West."[54] Here is a clear case of biased assimilation, in a way that promotes group polarization.

How can these findings be explained? And where and when do biased assimilation and attitude polarization occur?

Motivated Assimilations

The simplest point is that people appear to process information in a way that is distorted by their emotions and their motivations. Consider the well-established finding that after purchasing a product, people tend to seek out information confirming that their purchase was a sensible one. People are seeking to be reassured that they made the right decision. They wish to reduce cognitive dissonance, which makes people credit and seek out congruent information, and discredit and avoid incongruent information. More generally, people process information in a way that fits with their desires. They credit arguments that fit with what they already think, and they discredit arguments that point the other way.

Prior Convictions and Biases

Suppose that society consists of two groups of people, the Sensibles and the Haters, and that members of both groups have strong prior convictions. Suppose that the Sensibles have a strong antecedent commitment to a certain view— say, that the Holocaust actually happened, that Al Qaeda was responsible for the attacks of 9/11, that the president is not a Communist spy. Suppose that the Sensibles read balanced materials on these three questions.

The materials that support their antecedent view will not only seem convincing; they will also offer a range of details that will fortify the prior beliefs of most Sensibles. By contrast, the materials that contradict those beliefs will seem implausible, incoherent, ill-motivated, possibly a bit mad. The result is that people's antecedent convictions will be strengthened. Of course the opposite pattern will be observed for the Haters, who begin with the belief that the Holocaust did not happen, that the United States was itself responsible for the attacks on 9/11, that the president is a Communist spy. Biased assimilation can therefore be predicted from the mere existence of strong antecedent convictions and the effects of those convictions on (rational) judgments about new information.

When Biased Assimilation and When Not

This simple account helps to explain why biased assimilation will occur little, or perhaps not at all, if groups begin with a weak prior commitment. Suppose that the Sensibles are weakly committed to the propositions above and that the Haters disagree with them, but without much conviction. If both groups are exposed to balanced materials, they might tend to coalesce—at least if they do not have significantly asymmetrical trust.

Biased assimilation should be easy to understand in this light. It is in large part a product of strong prior convictions and also of divergences in trust. The Sensibles will trust some people and distrust others, and the Haters will show the opposite pattern. When they read materials from both sides, it is not exactly stunning that they end up learning from, and discounting, different sides. If, by contrast, people begin with weak prior convictions and do not suffer from asymmetrical trust, they will converge. We can also see in this light why people are often moved from their prior convictions, not by their usual antagonists and opponents, but by people with whom they typically identify.

Self-Defeating Corrections

Turn now to the case of correction. Suppose that people believe that the Holocaust did not happen and that Al Qaeda was not responsible for the attacks of 9/11. After reading materials that purport to be corrections, many people will be unlikely to change their views. On the contrary, the purported correction may be, in a sense, self-defeating. Perhaps the correction serves mostly to anger people; if so, it might strengthen their commitment to what they believed before. Perhaps the correction focuses people's attention on the issue and the debate in question, and in that sense leads them to commit themselves, more strongly than before, to what they vaguely believed. It is well established that when people are given information suggesting that they have no reason to fear what previously seemed to be a small risk, their fear often increases. This mysterious finding might be explained by the fact that the information focuses people's attention on that risk, and when attention is focused on a risk, fear increases. So too, perhaps, with corrections of false reports of wrongdoing: By focusing people's attention on those reports, they increase the sense that wrongdoing has occurred.

On purely cognitive grounds, it does seem harder to explain situations in which corrections actually strengthen (false) beliefs. But on certain assumptions, the very existence of the correction may attest to its falsehood. An attempted refutation by an untrustworthy source can be taken as additional evidence in favor of those beliefs. For example, the attempt might not have been made if the beliefs were not true. Why correct an error, unless there is not something to it?

Many corrections will of course not be self-defeating. If people do not have strong motivations for accepting a falsehood, if their prior knowledge is weak, and if they have a degree of trust in those who are providing the correction, then false beliefs will dissipate. Outcomes will thus be different among different social groups. Some groups will be strongly motivated, for example, to accept a terrible rumor about a politician or an institution, whereas other groups will be strongly motivated to reject it.

The Deliberative Opinion Poll

In some influential work, James Fishkin has pioneered the idea of a "deliberative opinion poll," in which small groups, consisting of highly diverse individuals, are asked to come together and deliberate about various issues.[55] Fishkin has conducted deliberative opinion polls on numerous questions and in several nations, including the United States, England, and Australia. Fishkin finds some noteworthy shifts in individual views, in a way that suggests that deliberation is having a significant effect, but he does not find a systematic tendency toward group polarization. In his studies, individuals shift both toward and away from the median of pre-deliberation views. In England, for example, deliberation led to reduced interest in using imprisonment as a tool for combating crime.[56] Similar shifts were shown in the direction of greater enthusiasm for procedural rights of defendants and increased willingness to explore alternatives to prison.[57]

On some issues, the effect of deliberation was to create an increase in the intensity with which people held their pre-existing convictions.[58] But in deliberative opinion polls, this was hardly a uniform pattern. On some questions, deliberation increased the percentage of people holding a minority position (with, for example, a jump from 36 percent to 57 percent of people favoring policies making divorce "harder to get").[59] These changes are very different from what we observed in Colorado, and they are not what would be predicted by group polarization.

How can we explain Fishkin's findings? At least three factors distinguish the deliberative opinion poll from standard tests of group polarization. First, Fishkin's groups were overseen by a moderator, concerned to ensure a level of openness and likely to alter some of the dynamics discussed here. Second, and probably more important, Fishkin's studies presented people with a set of written materials that tried to be balanced and that contained detailed arguments supporting sides. At least if people did not start with strong convictions, the likely result would be to move people in different directions from those that would be expected by simple group discussion, unaffected by external materials inevitably containing a degree of authority. Indeed, it would be easy to produce a set of such materials that would predictably shift people's views in the direction favored by the experimenter. And even without a self-conscious attempt at manipulation, or a general effort to be neutral and fair, the materials will undoubtedly affect the direction that deliberation will take group members.

Third, Fishkin's participants did not deliberate to a group decision, and the absence of such a decision probably weakened the influences that produce extremism. When people have committed themselves to a group judgment, it is likely that their individual responses, even if subsequent and anonymous, will be affected by the commitment. To be sure, group polarization has been found after mere exposure to the views of other group members, but it is typically smaller than after discussion and group judgment.[60] These three factors undoubtedly contribute to Fishkin's results.

GROUPS OVER TIME: "POLARIZATION GAMES"

Most studies of group polarization involve one-shot experiments. Consider, for example, the Colorado experiment, in which people were brought together, asked to talk, and then told to go home. Let us notice an intriguing implication of the experiments, an implication with special importance for people who meet with each other not once, but on a regular basis.

Suppose that participants engage in repeated discussions. Suppose that they meet each month, express views, and take votes. If so, there should be repeated shifts toward, and past, specific extreme points. Suppose that a group of citizens is thinking about genetic engineering of food, climate change, or the war on terror. The consequence of their discussions, over time, should be to lead in quite extreme directions. In these repeated *polarization games*, deliberation over time might well produce a situation in which people eventually come to hold positions more extreme than those of any individual member before the series of deliberations began.

In fact, the idea of repeated polarization games seems far more realistic than the processes studied in one-shot experiments. Groups typically meet many times, not just once. There appear to be few studies of such repeated polarization games. But it is not difficult to think of real-world groups in which the consequence of deliberation, over time, appears to be to shift both groups and individuals to positions that, early on, they could not possibly have accepted. Shifts of this kind clearly occurred with student groups in the 1960s.[61] They also seem to have occurred with Islamic terrorists in the aftermath of the attacks of 9/11.[62]

On the other hand, it is just not true that members of political organizations typically operate this way, even though they meet on a continuing basis. In the United States, Democrats do not usually move more and more to the left, and Republicans do not usually move more and more to the right. Why is this? One reason is that people are sensible and know what they think, or don't think, and their sense limits their movements. Another reason is the existence of *external constraints on extreme movements*. If Democrats shift far to the left, they will find themselves with fewer voters, and that fact imposes real discipline on the effects of internal deliberations. Political organizations are interested in attracting members and in achieving their goals, and this interest has significant limiting effects on potential movements. More generally, the direction and extent of extreme movements will often depend on the existence of external constraints. Market-type pressures, of the kind faced by political parties, often impose significant limits.

So, too, in the domain of business: Suppose that a group of people who lead a company go in an extreme direction. Suppose that the result is to produce inferior products. The company will be punished if consumers do not like those products. Life offers a number of reality checks, and these checks can limit shifts in our beliefs and our actions.

PEOPLE ARE DIFFERENT: OF THRESHOLDS AND TIPPING POINTS

Different people have different "thresholds" for moving as a result of new information or social pressure.[63] Such thresholds are important for understanding the dynamics of extremism.

Suppose that you believe that climate change is a serious problem and that the world should enter into an agreement to impose stringent limits on greenhouse gas emissions. It is possible that you hold this belief without much conviction, in the sense that if certain people told you that you were wrong, you might shift. Suppose several friends tell you that the best way to handle the problem of climate change is through modest limits on emissions that increase over time, alongside funds to help poor countries adapt to warmer climates. Perhaps their statements are enough to persuade you. If they are not, it may be because your threshold for changing your mind is very high, and you will not adopt a different view unless you are given detailed arguments from real authorities. The basic point is that some people will readily shift their views on hearing a different position, whereas others will shift with more difficulty, and still others will shift only when presented with truly overwhelming reasons to do so.

These points help to explain why different people will move in different degrees in a group setting, why some people will not move at all, and why some groups are more prone to major movement than others. Two things matter: the direction of people's original convictions and their thresholds for changing them. Recall that among federal judges, there is no polarization on the issues of abortion, national security, and capital punishment, apparently because the threshold for changing views is exceedingly high. When group members begin with firm convictions, they require a great deal of information or social pressure (or both) to change their views. If social influences are strong enough, such people will likely move, but the extent of their movement is limited because of relatively high thresholds for accepting certain beliefs or engaging in certain behavior.

Tipping points can be immensely important to extreme movements. Suppose, for example, that a group of people is deciding whether to undertake some action—say, to engage in violent protest. If only 10 percent of the group favors violent action and if majority rule is used, no violence will occur. But suppose that there are interdependencies among group members, so that what one person will do depends on what other people do. Suppose that people have diverse thresholds, and that most group members will opt to engage in violence if enough other members favor that course. If those who are clearly committed to violence make their views known at any early stage, others with relatively low thresholds will join them. If those with high thresholds resist and are sufficiently numerous, the first group will be outvoted. But suppose, instead, that there is a sequence in which the violence-prone state their views first, followed by those with low thresholds, and then followed by those with mildly higher thresholds. We could easily imagine a kind of cascade in the direction of violence.

The general point is that once a sufficient number of people converge on violence, a tipping point will occur, in the sense that those with higher thresholds will "tip," and eventually most group members will become willing to support violence. To know whether violence will occur, a great deal depends on who speaks or acts first, and also on the distribution of privately held views. It also follows that small and seemingly random variables can play a large role in moving large groups of people toward extremism.[64] Radical movements are sometimes impossible to predict, even though they seem inevitable in hindsight. The difficulty of prediction stems from the fact that observers do not have access to people's private thoughts and have no idea what kinds of thresholds would lead people to move in radical directions. The fall of communism had a great deal to do with processes of this kind.[65] When large changes occur that seemed unforeseeable, it is often because of diverse thresholds within the population. Once people start to shift, dramatic movements suddenly become possible.

AUTHORITY AND OBEDIENCE

Now let us turn to some of the most famous and most alarming findings in modern social science.[66] The experiments, conducted by the psychologist Stanley Milgram, involved influence not by the judgments of peers, but by the will of an experimenter. For better or for worse, these experiments almost certainly could not be performed today because of restrictions on the use of human subjects. But they are of independent interest, because they have large implications for social influences on judgments of both morality and facts. Indeed, it is not possible to understand extremism without understanding obedience, and it is not easy to understand obedience without understanding Milgram's work.

The experiments asked people to administer electric shocks to a person sitting in an adjacent room. Milgram's subjects were told, falsely, that the purpose of the experiments was to test people's memories and to see whether punishment might help people remember better. Unbeknownst to the subject, the victim of the electric shocks was a confederate, and there were no real shocks. The apparent shocks were delivered by a simulated shock generator with thirty clearly delineated voltage levels, ranging from 15 to 450 volts, accompanied by verbal descriptions ranging from "Slight Shock" to "Danger: Severe Shock." As the experiment unfolded, people were asked to administer increasingly severe shocks for incorrect answers to memory questions—with the shocks going to and past the "Danger: Severe Shock" level, which began at 400 volts.

In Milgram's original experiments, the subjects included forty men between the ages of twenty and fifty. They came from a range of occupations, including engineers, high school teachers, and postal clerks. They were paid a small amount for their participation—and also told that they could keep the money no matter how the experiment went. The "memory test" involved remembering word pairs; every mistake, by the confederate/victim, was to be met by an electric shock and a movement to one higher level on the shock generator. To ensure that everything seemed authentic, the subject was, at the beginning of the experiment, given an actual sample shock at the lowest level. But the subject was also assured that the shocks would not cause long-term harm, with the experimenter declaring, in response to a prearranged question from the confederate, "Although the shocks can be extremely painful, they cause no permanent tissue damage."[67]

In the original experiments, the victim did not make any protest until the 300-volt shock, when he loudly kicked the wall of the room where he was bound to the electric chair. After that point, the victim did not answer further questions and was heard from only after the 315-volt shock, when he pounded on the wall again—and was not heard from thereafter, even with increases in shocks to and past the 400-volt level. If the subject indicated an unwillingness to continue, the experimenter offered prods of increasing firmness, from "Please go on" to "You have no other choice; you *must* go on."[68] But the experimenter had no power to impose sanctions on subjects.

What do you think that people would do, when placed in this experiment? Most people predict that in such studies more than 95 percent of subjects would refuse to proceed to the end of the series of shocks. When people are asked to predict what people would do, the expected break-off point is "Very Strong Shock," 195 volts.[69] But in Milgram's original experiment, *every one of the forty subjects went beyond 300 volts.* The mean maximum shock level was 405 volts. A strong majority—twenty-six of forty, or 65 percent—went to the full 450-volt shock, two steps beyond "Danger: Severe Shock."[70]

Later variations on the original experiments produced even more remarkable results. In those experiments, the victim expressed a growing level of pain and distress as the voltage increased.[71] Small grunts were heard from 75 volts to 105 volts, and at 120 volts, the subject shouted, to the experimenter, that the shocks were starting to become painful. At 150 volts, the victim cries out, "Experimenter, get me out of here! I won't be in the experiment anymore! I refuse to go on!"[72] At 180 volts, the victim says, "I can't stand the pain." At 270 volts, he responds with an agonized scream. At 300 volts, he shouts that he will no longer answer the questions. At 315 volts, he screams violently. At 330 volts and after, he is not heard.

In this version of the experiment, there was no significant change in Milgram's results: Twenty-five of forty participants went to the maximum level, and the mean maximum level was above 360 volts. In a somewhat gruesome variation, the victim says, before the experiment begins, that he has a heart condition, and his pleas to discontinue the experiment include repeated references to the fact that his heart is "bothering" him as the shocks continue.[73] This, too, did not lead subjects to behave differently. Notably, women do not behave differently from men in these experiments; they show the same basic patterns of responses.

Milgram himself explains his results as involving obedience to authority, in a way that explains certain forms of extremism, including the behavior of Germans under Nazi rule. Indeed, Milgram conducted his experiments partly to

understand how the Holocaust could have happened.[74]
Milgram concluded that ordinary people will follow orders,
even if the result is to produce great suffering in innocent
others. Undoubtedly, simple obedience is part of the picture. But I want to urge an explanation that connects closely
with group polarization.[75]

The explanation involves the information conveyed by
the instructions of an apparently legitimate authority. People
who are invited to an academic setting, to participate in an
experiment run by an apparently experienced scientist,
might well defer to the experimenter's instructions, thinking
that the experimenter is likely to know what should be
done, all things considered, and that the experimenter is
not likely to inflict serious harm for no good reason. In
short, people are following a kind of heuristic or mental
shortcut: "If an experimenter had an established institution
asks me to do something, it is probably the right thing to do,
or at least not a terrible thing to do." If the experimenter asks
people to proceed, most of them might believe, reasonably,
that the harm apparently done to the victims is not serious
and that the experiment actually has significant benefits for
society. On this account, the experimenter has special
expertise. And on this account, many of the subjects put
their moral qualms to one side, not because of blind obedience, but because of a judgment that their qualms are likely
to have been ill-founded. That judgment must have been
based, in turn, on a belief that the experimenter is not likely
to ask subjects to proceed if the experiment is really objec-
tionable.

On this view, Milgram's subjects were responding to an
especially loud informational signal—the sort of signal sent
by a real specialist in the field. And note that in fact, those
who obeyed the authority, in Milgram's experiment, turned
out to be right: No suffering was inflicted. The serious

problem here, and what Milgram revealed, is that the heuristic—in favor of obedience of apparently trusted authorities—does not always work well. In real-world cases, it leads to terrible moral errors.

A subsequent study, exploring the grounds for obedience, offers support for this reading of Milgram's experiments.[76] In that study, a large number of people watched the tapes of those experiments and were asked to rank possible explanations for compliance with the experimenter's request. Deference to expertise was the highest-rank option. This is not definitive, of course, but an illuminating variation on the basic experiment, conducted by Milgram himself, provides further support.[77] In this variation, the subject was placed among *three* people asked to administer the shocks. Two of those people, actually Milgram's confederates, refused to go past a certain level (150 volts for one and 210 volts for the other). In such cases, the overwhelming majority of subjects—92.5 percent—defied the experimenter. This was by far the most effective of Milgram's many variations on his basic study, all designed to reduce the level of obedience.

It is clear that in Milgram's experiments, the influence came from the experimenter's own position—that the shocks should continue and that no permanent damage would be done. But when the subject's peers defied Milgram's experimenter, the experimenter's position was effectively negated by the information conveyed by the refusals of peers. Hence subjects could rely on their own moral judgments, or perhaps follow the moral signals indicated by the peers' refusals. Milgram himself established, in yet another variation, something nice about human nature. Without any advice from the experimenter and without any external influences at all, the subject's moral judgment was clear: *Do not administer shocks above a very low level.*[78]

The general lessons are straightforward. Group polarization occurs because of the informational and reputational signals given by others. When an authority tells people to do something, both of those signals can be very loud. If an authority tells you to do something apparently harmful or cruel, you might do exactly that, either because you think that it is the right thing to do or because you do not want to risk your reputation. In one experiment, for example, twenty of twenty-one nurses were willing to follow a doctor's orders to give a 20–milliliter dose of a drug called "androgen"—even though the label clearly stated that 5 milliliters was the usual dose and warned that 10 milliliters was the maximum.[79] Similar deference to authority can be found outside social science experiments. Almost half of surveyed nurses responded that they could remember a time when they had actually "carried out a physician's order that you felt could have had harmful consequences to the patient."[80]

In these cases, the nurses seemed to be following a sensible heuristic, to the following effect: "Follow doctors' orders, because doctors know what is in the best interest of patients." Under plausible assumptions, this heuristic also works pretty well. Medical care would probably be worse, not better, if nurses were regularly in the business of second-guessing the decisions of doctors. The problem, as in Milgram's experiments, is that the heuristic can produce significant errors. Doctors do blunder, and sometimes nurses would do better to make an inquiry.

Consider here the fact that no fewer than sixty-eight fast-food restaurants have been subject to successful strip-search scams, in which a male caller, masquerading as a police officer named Scott, informs an assistant store manager that an employee at the restaurant has committed theft.[81] Having learned a great deal about the local conditions, "Officer Scott" asks the manager for the name of an attractive female employee who, Scott says, has been engaged in theft and is likely to have contraband on her. Officer Scott is then allowed to talk to the employee, and he tells her that she has two choices. She can come to police headquarters to be strip-searched or instead be strip-searched at that very moment by a fellow employee. Believing herself to be innocent, the employee agrees. Officer Scott then instructs that fellow employee to search the young woman's most private places, with the store's video cameras looking on. This is a clear example of how a sensible heuristic, in favor of obedience to authority, can go badly wrong. People should usually obey police officers—but not when they ask women to submit to a strip-seach for no legitimate purpose.

The case of Officer Scott is a scam, of course, but it suggests that extreme movements often occur simply because someone in a position of authority has initiated them. Real atrocities, including torture and even genocide, can be explained in part by reference to mechanisms of this sort.[82] Consider these words from a participant in the genocide in Rwanda: "When you receive a new order, you hesitate but you obey, or else you're taking a risk. When you have been prepared the right way by the radios and the official advice, you obey more easily, even if the order is to kill your neighbors. The mission of a good organizer is to stifle your hesitations when he gives you instructions ... You obey freely."[83] And after a time, what was required may become in the nature of habit. As another put it, "At first killing was obligatory; afterward we got used to it. We became naturally cruel. We no longer needed encouragement or fines to kill, or even orders or advice. Discipline was relaxed because it wasn't necessary anymore."[84]

There is an important point here about the nature of ordinary moral inhibitions and the importance of strengthening the moral intuitions that underlie them. As Tzvetan Todorov writes, "What the crimes of the Nazis teach us is that those who enforce the law are more dangerous than those who break it. If only the guards had given themselves over to their instincts! Unfortunately, they followed the rules."[85] In his account, the predominant type of guard in the concentration camps was "a conformist, willing to serve whoever wielded power and more concerned with his own welfare than with the triumph of doctrine."[86] When the system is working well, prison guards usually should obey their superiors, but when the system is not working well, they should be prepared to disobey.

SITUATIONISM, PRISON ABUSE, AND THE STANFORD PRISON EXPERIMENT

These points suggest two different answers to a perennial question: Why do human beings commit despicable acts? One answer points to individual dispositions; a different answer, suggested by Milgram's work, emphasizes situational pressures. In 2005, Secretary of State Condoleezza Rice stressed the importance of individual dispositions in describing terrorists as "simply evil people who want to kill." So-called situationists reject this view. They believe that horrible acts can be committed by perfectly normal people. The most extreme situationists insist that in the right circumstances, most of us, and perhaps almost all of us, might be led to commit atrocities.

The situationist view receives strong support from Milgram's experiment, from studies of group polarization, and also from Philip Zimbardo's influential study of situational influences, known as the Stanford Prison Experiment.[87]

Because Zimbardo's experiment bears on extreme behavior in multiple domains, it will be useful to spend some time with it here.

The experiment started with an ad in a local newspaper, asking for volunteers for a study of prison life, lasting two weeks and paying $15 a day (about $75 in current dollars). Seventy of those who answered the ad were called to Stanford for interviews and a series of psychological tests. All seventy were American college students; most had completed summer school courses at Stanford or Berkeley. Twenty-four of them were selected on the ground that they were the healthiest and most normal. Half were randomly assigned to be prison guards; the other half were randomly assigned to be prisoners. All of them indicated that they would prefer to be prisoners, in part because they could not imagine being a prison guard after college, but they could imagine being in jail, and they thought they might learn from the experience. All of them agreed to participate through informed consent forms. They were also informed that if they were assigned the role of prisoners, they would suffer deprivations of their civil rights and have only minimally adequate diet and medical care. Those assigned to be prisoners were also told to wait at home on a particular Sunday, when they would be contacted to begin the experiment.

On that day, they were surprised to find themselves "arrested" by actual Stanford police officers (enlisted by Zimbardo), who handcuffed them, searched them, advised them of their rights, and booked them at police headquarters. Brought to a mock prison in the basement of the Stanford psychology department, they were stripped, deloused, and made to wear smocks, without underwear, and with numbers sewn on front and back. They were also forced to wear ankle chains and nylon stocking caps (not having been asked to shave their heads). They walked in uncomfortable rubber thongs. Having worked with one of Zimbardo's graduate students, the guards read the prisoners a series of rules: "prisoners will be allowed 5 minutes in the lavatory," "prisoners must address each other by number only," "prisoners must never refer to their condition as an 'experiment' or a 'simulation,' " and others. Somewhat ominously, prisoners were told that the last rule was the most important: "Failure to obey any of the above rules may result in punishment."

The first day of the experiment was awkward for guards and prisoners alike, and not terribly eventful. Some of the guards did seem to relish their role, asking prisoners to do push-ups as "punishment" for laughing at some of the guards' comments. Whenever a prisoner showed an irreverent attitude, he was likely to be asked to do more push-ups. Some guards engaged in acts of arbitrary cruelty—say, by leaning on prisoners and pushing them back with billy clubs. Things got much worse on Monday. On that day, the prisoners staged a rebellion, ripping off their numbers, refusing to obey commands, and mocking the guards.

Zimbardo asked the guards to take steps to control the situation. They did exactly that. Their responses consisted of forcing the prisoners to do jumping jacks and push-ups; stripping them naked in their cells; depriving them of meals, pillows, blankets, and beds; and placing them in solitary confinement. Some of the prisoners were baffled by the sheer aggressiveness of the response, with one screaming wildly, "No, no, no! This is an *experiment*! Leave me alone! Shit, let go of me, fucker! You're not going to take our fucking beds!" The rebellion was effectively crushed.

As the behavior of the guards became increasingly aggressive and humiliating, one of the prisoners, named

Doug, broke down and asked to be released. Zimbardo, having adopted the role of "prison superintendent," met with him privately. Zimbardo told Doug that he would forfeit his payment if he quit early, asked him to serve as an informer in return for "special privileges," and generally convinced him to continue. Returning to the prison, Doug falsely announced to the other prisoners that they could not leave. Shortly thereafter, his own stress reactions appeared to become hysterical, even pathological, as he threatened violence against both the guards and himself, and he was indeed released. On each of the next three days, another prisoner showed acute stress reactions and had to be released. The remaining prisoners became subdued and "zombie-like."

What of the guards? The picture was one of growing cruelty, aggression, and dehumanization. Sometimes without provocation, the guards stripped the prisoners naked, hooded them, chained them, denied them food or bedding privileges, put them into solitary confinement, and made them clean toilet bowls with their bare hands. There was sexual humiliation as well. On Thursday, one of the most aggressive guards, nicknamed John Wayne, called out to several of the prisoners, "See that hole in the ground? Now do twenty-five push-ups, *fucking* that hole! You hear me!" The prisoners dutifully obeyed. He continued, "Now, you two, you're male camels. Stand behind the female camels and *hump* them." Submitting to the order, the prisoners simulated sodomy.

The experiment ended prematurely after Zimbardo enlisted the help of Christina Maslach, a recent Stanford PhD in psychology who was starting her career as an assistant professor at Berkeley. In Maslach's own words, "I looked at the line of hooded, shuffling, chained prisoners, with guards shouting orders at them ... I was overwhelmed by a chilling, sickening feeling." Refusing to engage Zimbardo's claim that this was "amazing stuff," Maslach ended up in a heated argument with him (notwithstanding the fact that they were romantically involved at the time). She describes the "fight" as "too long and too traumatic," but eventually Zimbardo acknowledged that the experiment had had an adverse effect on him, as well as on the student subjects. He decided to halt the experiment on Friday.

Zimbardo himself draws some large lessons from his experiment. He insists that individual dispositions are far less important than we tend to think and that situational pressures can lead decent people to commit terrible acts. Recall that the prisoners and the guards were randomly assigned to their roles. "The line between Good and Evil, once thought to be impermeable, proved instead to be quite permeable."[88] Those assigned to be prisoners behaved as prisoners and were in a sense broken by the role. Those assigned to be as guards behaved badly, even viciously, notwithstanding their general normality. Zimbardo writes, "At the start of this experiment, there were no differences between the two groups; less than a week later, there were no similarities between them."[89] Notably, the prisoners were skeptical of the claim of random assignment and insisted, after the conclusion of the experiment, that the guards were taller than they were. (They were wrong; the two groups had the same average height.)

In pointing to the apparent normality of those involved in Nazi war crimes, Zimbardo gives a social science twist to Hannah Arendt's claims about the "banality of evil." And in explaining what makes atrocities possible, Zimbardo places a large emphasis on deindividuation—a process by which both perpetrators and victims become essentially anonymous and are thereby transformed into a type or a role. The very decision to wear a uniform can have significant behavioral effects; warriors who change their appearance in preparation for war are more likely to brutalize their enemies. During the process of deindividuation, people enter a state of arousal in which they do not face the ordinary social sanctions and in which their own moral doubts are silenced. In this account, deindividuation ensures the triumph of "the Dionysian trait of uninhibited release and lust" over the "Apollonian central trait" of "constraint and the inhibition of desire."[90]

These general points, and the Stanford Prison Experiment in particular, seem to help to explain the horrific behavior of American soldiers at Abu Ghraib. Recall the well-publicized incidents, some of them photographed, in which soldiers humiliated prisoners by leading them around by dog leashes, forcing them to simulate fellatio, and making them masturbate in front of a cigarette-smoking female soldier (herself giving a high-five salute of approval). American personnel also threatened male detainees with rape, beat them with broom handles and chairs, punched and kicked them, and forced them to wear women's underwear. Perhaps such abuses were a predictable consequence of situational forces, not (as prominent military leaders have urged) of the dispositions of rogue soldiers or a few bad apples.

In the Stanford Prison Experiment, the most interesting puzzle is the behavior of the guards. How could ordinary college students show such a high level of aggression and cruelty? It is true that unlike in the Milgram experiments, no authority was issuing specific orders. But Zimbardo specifically instructed guards to assume a particular role, in which they "have total power" with the task of producing "the required psychological state in the prisoners for as long as the study lasted." Zimbardo, a professor at Stanford, told college students to make the students "feel as though they were in prison." These instructions, alongside the very role of the guard, conveyed certain information about what should be done. Those who find themselves operating as prison guards know that they should behave in certain ways. This is no less true in an experimental setting than elsewhere. Indeed, the experimental setting might have aggravated the behavior of some of the guards, who knew that certain safeguards were in place and that their specific task was to induce "the required psychological state."

We might draw some large lessons from this conclusion. Perhaps those who engage in extreme behavior are led to do so by their role and their context; perhaps all of us, under certain circumstances, could commit atrocities. Chillingly, Milgram himself said, "If a system of death camps were set up in the United States of the sort that we had seen in Nazi Germany, one would be able to find sufficient personnel for those camps in any medium-sized American town."[91]

At Abu Ghraib in Iraq, otherwise ordinary members of the military, both male and female, understood various forms of torture and humiliation as "standard operating procedure."[92] Sabrina Harman, a soldier who famously appeared in photographs in which prisoners were sexually humiliated, observed, "That's the only way to get through each day, to start blocking things out. Just forget what happened. You go to bed, and then you have the next day to worry about. It's another day closer to home. Then that day's over, and you just block that one out."[93] Tim Dugan, another soldier, said that the soldiers were told, " 'We got a chance to break this unlawful insurgency, and the people in an unlawful insurgency have no protection under the Geneva Conventions.' ... If the fuckin' secretary of defense designates the motherfucker an unlawful insurgency, I mean, what the fuck am I supposed to say? It's an unlawful insurgency, wouldn't you think? He's the second-highest motherfucker in the country during the war."[94]

Alison Des Forges, an investigator of the Rwandan genocide with Human Rights Watch, concluded:

> This behavior lies just under the surface of any of us. The simplified accounts of genocide allow distance between us and the perpetrators of genocide. They are so evil we couldn't ever see ourselves doing the same thing. But if you consider the terrible pressure under which people were operating, then you automatically reassert their humanity—and that becomes alarming. You are forced to look at the situation and say, "What would I have done?" Sometimes the answer is not encouraging.[95]

Des Forges is undoubtedly right, and the behavior of American soldiers at Abu Ghraib supports her point. Of special note, for purposes of understanding that behavior, is the fact that the soldiers did not learn the prisoners' names; on the contrary, they gave them nicknames, turning them into "cartoon characters, which make them comfortably unreal."[96] In the words of one of the soldiers: "I had one guy whose breath just stank. I called him Yuck Mouth. We had a guy—probably the tallest Iraqi I've ever seen—and his nose kind of looked like Big Bird off Sesame Street. I called him Big Bird. I had Trap Jaw, because he had real sharp teeth, looked like he could chew a brick. I had one that I called Gomer Pyle."[97] This kind of deindividuation of the victims of abuse is characteristic of what happens when people are asked to play certain social roles.

But for purely situational accounts of human behavior, there is an evident problem. The Stanford Prison Experiment uncovered significant differences among both prisoners and guards. Some of the prisoners could not handle the situation and essentially screamed, "Let me out of here!"—in part, perhaps, as a strategic effort to escape a terrible situation. Some of the guards did their jobs, but without cruelty, and they did various favors for the prisoners. These identifiably "good guards" were altogether different from others, whose behavior was sadistic. Dispositions did matter. There is a real difference between the actual perpetrators and those who simply stood by. The same is true of American soldiers at Abu Ghraib, with a few enthusiastic about acts of abuse, and a few others seeming to revel in them. Sometimes one of the solders "would see something happening with a prisoner, and say, 'Hey, this is wrong,' or, 'Operationally, we can't do this.' But when they said nothing," the worst of the soldiers would feel free to act.[98] And recall, too, that Christina Maslach, the assistant professor involved in a romantic relationship with Zimbardo, expressed outrage and asked for the experiment to end, notwithstanding the obvious pressure simply to go along, and perhaps to marvel. As Zimbardo himself emphasizes, many human beings are able to resist situational pressures and to engage in forms of heroism. Even when group polarization is under way, some people, some of the time, will hold fast to their convictions and stay where they are, especially if group members go in destructive or violent directions.

Here is one way to think about the Stanford Prison Experiment and its real-world analogues, which might help us to sort out the relationship between dispositions and social contexts. In experimental settings and in the real world, most people will be reluctant to harm others. Most of them have strong moral commitments, and it will not be so easy for the situation to lead them to put those commitments to one side. Often their reluctance can be overcome with appropriate incentives and the right information. If people can be assured that any harm is small or nonexistent, or necessary to produce some greater good, they might well put their moral qualms to one side. (Recall Milgram's experiments.) If people can be assured that any harm is deserved, or part of legitimate punishment, then they might well be willing to inflict harm. (Prison guards do not refuse to put recalcitrant prisoners in solitary confinement.) But—and this is the key point—different people have radically different thresholds that must be met before they will be willing to harm others. Even at Abu Ghraib, there were significant differences in the attitudes and the behavior of American soldiers who lived in a situation that encouraged cruelty and apparent sadism. Some soldiers even turned out to be heroes, alerting the authorities to what was happening. Studies of genocide show disparities as well, even when killing is pervasive. As one killer recalled, "We became more and more cruel, more and more calm, more and more bloody. But we did not see that we were becoming more and more killers. The more we cut, the more cutting became child's play to us. For a few, it turned into a treat, if I may say so."[99]

Some people—life's "bad guards"—have a real capacity for sadism and cruelty; that capacity is built into their dispositions. If such people are instructed to act sadistically, or merely authorized to do so, they will. Other people have somewhat higher thresholds. They will require strong situational assurance that harming others is justified or acceptable, all things considered. Still other people—life's heroes or those who refuse to act in accordance with role and culture that lead most people in terrible directions—have exceedingly high thresholds, or perhaps their moral convictions operate as an absolute barrier. The resistance of the heroes seems to be a product of a deeply engrained moral sense, whose roots are not well understood, but which undoubtedly comes, for many people, from background factors that enable or even require people to say a firm: "No!" A continuum of thresholds exists from the sadists to the heroes, or from the devils to the saints.

If all of this is right, we can understand why different prison experiments, and different prisons, might have different outcomes. A great deal depends on the initial mix of dispositions. A group of low-threshold guards will behave very differently from a group of high-threshold guards, in part because of their antecedent inclinations, and in part because of social interactions among them. Because of group polarization, a set of low-threshold guards might well become very cruel indeed, whereas a set of high-threshold guards will probably behave pretty well. With mixed groups, we could easily imagine a range of outcomes, ranging from extreme cruelty to comparative generosity. If the low-threshold guards act first and influence their high-threshold colleagues, cruelty is likely; if the high-threshold guards act first and influence the low-threshold types, the outcome will be much better. If heroes are present, and if they are clear and confident, they might be able to ensure a good outcome. Hierarchical relationships at many organizations—including schools, workplaces, and religious organizations—can be understood in roughly analogous terms. Teachers, employers, and religious leaders can take on some of the characteristics of aggressive prison guards, or not, and individual thresholds and social interactions make all the difference.

A great deal depends as well on the specific incentives and on existing information. Most low-threshold types will not show cruelty unless they are given at least some incentive to do so. Those with relatively high thresholds might be willing to show considerable aggression if their incentives are strong enough. Of course, beliefs can have a significant impact. Suppose that people are informed that aggression is justified or necessary in the circumstances. Perhaps they learn, or are told, that the victims of their aggression are wrongdoers who deserve whatever they get. Or perhaps they learn that they are a part of a group of people (ethnic, religious, national) who have been systematically humiliated by others and who are entirely justified in responding to past humiliation. Or perhaps they learn that certain individuals or certain groups are bad by disposition, or perhaps even subhuman, and must be treated accordingly. Dispositions are partly a product of beliefs, contributing to low or high thresholds, and once belief-driven dispositions are in place, social situations can add fresh information, often overcoming the relevant threshold.

What emerges is a clear challenge to the most ambitious claims for situationism and a more complicated understanding of the relationship between individual dispositions and social situations. That understanding fits the Stanford Prison Experiment, and it helps to explain why different social contexts, and different social roles, can produce such radically diverse results.

The prison experiment shows that the very assumption of a particular social role automatically conveys a great deal of information about appropriate behavior. But social roles are not fixed. Prison guards need not feel free to brutalize prisoners. Perhaps the largest lesson is that a constant sense of moral responsibility should be taken to be a part of, rather than inconsistent with, a wide range of social roles.

A NOTE ON THE INTERNET—AND THE ARCHITECTURE OF SERENDIPITY

Many people have expressed concern about the social influences that are exerted via the mass media and the Internet.[100] Perhaps some of these influences produce unjustified extremism. A general problem is one of fragmentation, or "cyberbalkanization." The Internet is making it possible for people to design a kind of Daily Me—their personal communications packages, which include only the topics and opinions that they like and exclude troublesome issues and disfavored voices. With greater specialization, people are increasingly able to avoid general interest newspapers and magazines and to make choices that reflect their own predispositions. Many people appear to be hearing more and louder versions of their own views, thus reducing the benefits that come from exposure to competing views and unnoticed problems. Long before the Internet, it was possible to discuss the "racial stratification of the public sphere" by reference to divergences between white and African American newspapers.[101] The Internet creates a much more dramatic "stratification," as groups of multiple kinds can sort themselves into like-minded types.

We should be clear about the nature of the problem. In any free society, you can read and see what you like, and you are allowed to exclude the rest. But with daily newspapers and evening news shows, we often live with a kind of *architecture of serendipity*—that is, a situation in which we will have a number of serendipitous encounters with topics and points of view. These encounters can have a large impact; sometimes they can even change our lives.

We might think, for example, that we have no interest in some problem in Turkey or India, but a story on these nations might spark our interest and divert our attention, possibly prompting action. We might think that we have a certain view on climate change or on labor unions, but a story might suggest that our thoughts are badly wrong and that we should consider a different perspective. If the architecture of serendipity is transformed into an architecture of control, people may well restrict themselves to topics and views that they find congenial.

In a way, of course, this is freedom in action. But an understanding of group polarization explains why a fragmented communications market may create serious problems. If people on the Internet are deliberating mostly with like-minded others, their views will not merely be reinforced; they will instead be shifted to more extreme points. Indeed, the Internet would seem to be replicating the Colorado experiment, and doing so every hour of every day. With the Internet, it is exceedingly easy for each of us to find like-minded types. Views that would ordinarily dissolve, simply because of an absence of social support, can be found in large numbers on the Internet, even if they are understood to be exotic, indefensible, or bizarre in most communities. As Marc Sageman writes, "Let's assume that a very few people in the world share the same strange belief, say, that the moon is made of green cheese. Through a process of self-selection, they find each other on the same forum. . . . Soon, they will assume that everyone shares this conviction because only the true believers air their views and the rest stay silent."[102] Recall that group polarization sometimes occurs because people do not take sufficient account of the fact that the views of group members are biased, or worse, and do not really represent the convictions of most people in the community. The problem is especially severe on the Internet, where it is so easy to find support for judgments that are held by only a (bizarre, confused, or hateful) few.

This point is strengthened by the fact, noted previously, that polarization is all the greater and all the more likely when people are attached by bonds by affection, common ality, or solidarity. Many Internet discussion groups are unified by a sense of shared identity. Hence a "plausible hypothesis is that the Internet-like setting is most likely to create a strong tendency toward group polarization when the members of the group feel some sense of group identity."[103] Here as elsewhere, this cannot be said to be bad by itself. Perhaps the increased extremism is good. But it is certainly troublesome if diverse social groups are led, through predictable mechanisms, toward increasingly opposing and ever more extreme views. Mutual misunderstandings, even anger and contempt, are nearly inevitable.

In the modern era, terrorism is the most dramatic example. In Sageman's words, the "structure of the Internet has become the structure of global Islamic terrorism. It has evolved organically through the search and exploration of new safe methods of interaction by thousands of terrorist sympathizers given the fact that their physical habitat had become very hostile post-9/11."[104] Until 2004, face-to-face interactions played the key role in producing terrorist networks. More recently, the Internet has assumed great importance. Sageman emphasizes that the traditional hierarchy of terrorist groups is undermined by the Internet, which leads to a form of spontaneous self-organization. Chat rooms and dedicated forums help to inspire many young Muslims to join the Islamic terrorist movement. "The new forums have the same influence that these radical mosques played in the previous generation of terrorists."[105] Conspiracy theories, fueling outrage, are spread in rapid fashion, as "individuals seek and select the rooms most compatible with their views and abandon the ones they disagree with. In a sense, the followers vote with their mice and select the views they like."[106] In the context of terrorism, a kind of "leaderless Jihad" is a result. "Thanks to the Internet, global Islamic terrorism may fade away, but will never completely die."[107]

This is an extreme example. But in countless domains, the Internet produces a process of spontaneous creation of groups of like-minded types, fueling group polarization. People who would otherwise be loners, or isolated in their objections and concerns, congregate into social networks.

HOMOPHILY AND CURIOSITY

Of course, it is true that people are curious, and many of us actually like serendipity. We seek, and do not deplore, a situation in which we are exposed to new ideas and competing views. In our own way, we combat group polarization, simply because we resist information cocoons and groups that consist solely of like-minded types. In business and in government, successful leaders seek divergent views and fresh opinions, precisely because of their intuitive awareness of the risks of polarization. In the United States, Presidents Abraham Lincoln and Franklin Delano Roosevelt are the foremost examples; they made special efforts to ensure that they did not live in echo chambers. It turns out that humility and curiosity help to ensure better decisions, in large part because they increase the pool of information. The Internet can help to prevent polarization if people use it to find novel points of view. In many societies, group polarization is countered, every day, by people's desire to test their own judgments against those of dissimilar others.

Nonetheless, there does seem to be a strong human tendency to self-segregate along the kinds of lines that promote polarization. In sociology, a detailed empirical literature explores "homophily"—the process by which "similarity breeds connection."[100] People who are similar along relevant dimensions tend to seek out one another and to live in the same social networks. In small groups, people who are unified by such demographic characteristics as age, education, race, religion, and ethnicity show a distinct tendency to self-segregate. The same is true of those unified along the lines of aspirations, attitudes, and intelligence. For present purposes, what is most important is "value homophily," which includes the "considerable tendency for adults to associate with those of their own political affiliation."[109] Within the United States, many people believe that most sensible people share their political convictions, if only because those with whom they associate tend to think as they do.

Why does homophily occur? As a matter of history, geography has played a large role. Family, work, and other organizations also create strong ties among like-minded types. But these structural sources are complemented by voluntary ties and personal choices. People of similar religious views often choose to associate with one another. The hostility between believers and nonbelievers is in part a product of polarization. Miller McPherson and colleagues find that in many domains, "attraction is affected by perceived similarity," and people "associate with similar others for ease of communication, shared cultural tastes, and other features that smooth the coordination of activity and communication."[110] In the era of the Internet, a great deal of work remains to be done on the extent to which homophily is creating niches of like-minded types. But a lot of evidence supports the view that cultural tastes, including tastes for music, spread through a process involving homophily.[111] To a large degree, people's tastes are shaped through interaction with others who have similar inclinations.[112] What is true for cultural preferences is undoubtedly true for political judgments and risk attitudes as well.

Existing work on homophily has not been brought into contact with the phenomenon of group polarization. This is a serious gap. It is clear that if birds of a feather are flocking together, extreme movements are to be expected. What is important is that the extent of the flocking depends both on social architecture and on prevailing norms. If people naturally encounter those who are unlike themselves, or if workplaces and media facilitate such encounters, homophily will be counteracted. And if social norms encourage people to cultivate the tendency toward curiosity, and even to delight in new topics and opinions, then groups will contain birds of many different feathers.

GROUPTHINK AND GROUP POLARIZATION

We are now in a position to assess groupthink, a widely discussed phenomenon in the 1970s and 1980s, one that bears directly on my concerns here. Developed by Irving Janis, the idea of groupthink is designed to capture processes of decision that predictably lead to social blunders, catastrophes, and even forms of extremism.[113] Janis's term drew directly and self-consciously on George Orwell's *1984* and, in particular, on Orwell's term *doublethink*. Stated briefly, Janis's suggestion was that certain groups stifle dissent, value consensus over correctness, fail to examine alternatives and consequences, and as a result, end up producing fiascoes. Janis's plea was for a process of decision that would be "vigilant" in the sense that it would ensure careful attention to alternative courses of action and to the risks associated with those alternatives.

To support his argument, Janis relied on a number of actual policy decisions. According to Janis, groupthink was largely responsible for President Kennedy's disastrous decision to authorize the Bay of Pigs invasion. When President Johnson and his advisers escalated the Vietnam War during 1964–67, it was because the relevant group stifled dissent, sought consensus, and did not think well about consequences. The idea of groupthink has been applied to the Watergate cover-up,[114] Neville Chamberlain's policy of appeasing Nazi Germany,[115] the Ford Motor Company's

decision to market the Edsel, NASA's launch of the
Challenger space shuttle, Nazi Germany's invasion of the
Soviet Union in 1941, and the decision by Chemie Gru-
nenthal to market thalidomide, which caused serious birth
defects in children.[116] President George W. Bush's decision
to launch the Iraq war can easily be understood in terms of
groupthink.[117] In Janis's view, groupthink leads to many
problems of defective decision making, including incom-
plete survey of alternatives and objectives, failure to examine
the risks of the preferred choice, poor information search,
selective bias in processing information, and failure to assess
alternatives.[118]

Janis argued that groupthink involves several "types" of
symptoms.[119] These include close-mindedness, involving a
collective effort "to rationalize" so as to discount warnings
or information that might lead to reconsideration, and
stereotyped views of enemies, as either too evil to warrant
efforts at negotiation or "too weak and stupid to counter"
the group's risky choices. Organizations susceptible to
groupthink impose pressures toward uniformity. Here Janis
refers to self-censorship on the part of group members, who
minimize the importance of their own doubts and counterarguments. Self-censorship is connected with an illusion of
unanimity. This illusion is fostered by direct pressure on any
members who argue against the group's stereotypes, illusions, and commitments.

Janis added that groupthink has a set of identifiable causes.
The first and most important is cohesiveness; a group that
lacks that quality is not "likely to display symptoms of
defective decision-making." But groupthink requires additional conditions. These include insulation of the policy-
making group, which reduces the chance of receiving expert
advice and critical evaluation from outside; lack of a tradition of impartial leadership, meaning that leaders will not

encourage open inquiry and critical evaluation; lack of procedures for promoting good decision making; and homogeneous social backgrounds and ideology on the part of members.

Janis contended that the remedy for groupthink involves vigilant processing of information.[120] Leaders should encourage critical evaluation by giving high priority to objections and doubts. To promote diversity of view, independent policy-planning and evaluation groups should work on the same problems, with different leaders. Group members should be assigned the role of devil's advocate, bringing a new perspective to bear. Outside experts and qualified people not directly involved in the issue at hand should be encouraged to challenge prevailing views. In support of these ideas, Janis found that groupthink was absent in many successful decisions, such as the Kennedy administration's peaceful resolution of the Cuban Missile Crisis and the Marshall Plan for rebuilding Europe after World War II.

How do Janis's claims bear on my argument here? I have emphasized that groups can go to extremes. I have also urged that social pressures, both informational and reputational, are heightened if group members have a high degree of solidarity and affection. In this light, many of Janis's examples can be seen as case studies in group polarization, as groups move to more extreme points in line with their original tendencies. Janis's emphasis on self-censorship, heightened by social pressures, fits well with my basic claims. As he shows, many examples of group polarization require an appreciation of the role of leaders, whose views count for far more than those of other group members. If a leader does not encourage dissent and is inclined to an identifiable conclusion, it is highly likely that the group as a whole will move toward that conclusion.

In my view, the idea of group polarization is far more helpful, in explaining both extremism and error, than the idea of groupthink. It should be clear that Janis does not suggest any simple hypothesis that might be tested. Empirical work on the groupthink phenomenon has suggested a mixed verdict,[121] and there is a lively debate over Janis's claims.[122] Much of the debate stems from uncertainty about the relationship between Janis's claimed symptoms and policy fiascoes. Critics have urged that that "support for the posited groupings of groupthink characteristics derives from anecdote, casual observation, and intuitive appeal rather than rigorous research."[123]

A careful study of successful and unsuccessful decision making in seven prominent American companies (including Chrysler, Coca-Cola, and CBS News) tried to test whether such companies exhibit groupthink and, if so, whether a lack of success is correlated with it.[124] In support of Janis's claims, the authors did find a strong relationship between a group's decision-making process and its likelihood of success. When information was processed well, companies were more likely to make good decisions. On the other hand, the successful groups showed some features of groupthink. In fact, those groups had strong leaders who attempted to persuade others that they were right. Such leaders produced mistakes only if they created "absolutist cults," defined as organizations centralizing power in a single person.[125] Such centralization, more than anything else, is associated with bad outcomes.

This study finds analogues in many others that have found some, but not complete, support for the groupthink model.[126] A systematic exploration of Janis's own examples concluded that groupthink characteristics were indeed correlated with failures.[127] In particular, the study found that defective decision making was strongly correlated with the

structural faults of groups, including insulation and homo-
geneity. But when group members are friends rather than
strangers, have worked together in the past, or are asked
to wear group labels, they have not shown more self-
censorship than other groups, and it is not at all clear
that such cohesive groups make worse decisions.[128] It
may well be that if members trust one another and share
norms of disclosure and dissent, there will be less self-
censorship than in groups of strangers, for in such groups,
people might fear that a dissident view will create serious
friction.

But some of Janis's claims have fared well. Insulated
groups have been found to consider fewer alternatives and
make worse decisions that noninsulated groups.[129] Also in
support of Janis's claims, groups with highly directive leaders
have been found to suggest fewer alternatives, to use less
information, to suppress dissent, and generally to show
inferior decision-making processes.[130] Most studies also
find that poor decision-making procedures, under Janis's
criteria, produce less disagreement and worse decisions
than do good procedures.[131]

How do all these findings bear on the analysis here? What
is the relationship between groupthink and group polarization? The most obvious point is that group polarization
offers a simple and clear prediction: As a statistical regularity,
deliberating groups will end up in a more extreme point in
line with their predeliberation tendencies. The idea of
groupthink is far more complex and unruly, without any
simple predictions. Working from real-world examples,
Janis generalized a set of points about when groups are
most likely to blunder. The generalizations are suggestive
and helpful, but they do not offer a clear account of what
characteristics of groups will lead to extremism, blunders, or
catastrophes.

CASCADES

My emphasis thus far has been on group polarization. But extremism can also be fueled by a closely related phenomenon: *social cascades*. As cascades occur, beliefs and perspectives spread from some people to others, to the point where many people are relying, not on what they actually know, but on what (they think) other people think. This belief may well be erroneous, because people are relying not on their private information, but on the judgments of trusted others. When people conclude that the United States or Israel was responsible for the attacks of 9/11, or that doctors were responsible for the spread of AIDS among African Americans, or that a certain investment can't miss, cascades are typically responsible. Cascades play a large role in the stock market and in real estate. When certain stocks become suddenly popular, cascades are usually involved.[132] Companies do their best to create cascades; the iPhone and the iPod are both terrific products, but they have definitely benefited from cascade effects. When people are suddenly fearful of a new risk, cascades are usually fueling their fear. Conspiracy theories in general tend to spread from one person to another through a cascade-like process. Social cascades come in two varieties: informational and reputational.

Informational Cascades

To see how informational cascades work, imagine a deliberating group that is deciding whether some person or group has engaged in unfair or even outrageous conduct, warranting some kind of punishment or reprisal.[133] Assume that the group members are announcing their views in sequence. From his own knowledge and experience, each member has some private information about what that person or group has done. But each member also attends, reasonably enough, to the judgments of others.

Andrews is the first to speak. He suggests that bad conduct has indeed occurred. Barnes now knows Andrews's judgment; it is clear that she, too, should certainly conclude that there is unfairness if she agrees independently with Andrews. But if her independent judgment is otherwise, she would—if she trusts Andrews no more and no less than she trusts herself—be indifferent about what to think or do, and she might simply flip a coin. Now turn to a third person, Carlton. Suppose that both Andrews and Barnes have said that outrageous conduct has occurred, but that Carlton's own information, though not conclusive, suggests that they are wrong. In that event, Carlton might well ignore what he knows and follow Andrews and Barnes. It is likely, after all, that both Andrews and Barnes had reasons for their conclusion, and unless Carlton thinks that his own information is better than theirs, he should follow their lead. If he does, Carlton is in a cascade.

Now suppose that Carlton is speaking in response to what Andrews and Barnes did, not on the basis of his own information, and also that later people, in our little queue, know what Andrews, Barnes, and Carlton said. On reasonable assumptions, they will do exactly what Carlton did. That is, they will agree that outrageous conduct has occurred, regardless of their private information (which, we are supposing, is relevant but inconclusive). This will happen even if Andrews initially blundered. That initial blunder, in short, can start a process by which a number of people participate in creating serious mistakes.

If this is what is happening, there is a major social problem: People who are in the cascade do not disclose the information that they privately hold. In the example just given, the judgment of group members will not reflect the overall knowledge, or the aggregate knowledge, of those within the group—even if the information held by individual members, if actually revealed and aggregated, would produce a better and quite different conclusion. The reason for the problem is that individuals are following the lead of those who came before. And if people are doing this, then they might end up in quite extreme directions. They might also converge on a judgment about climate change, or the right investments, or Iran, or China, or the intentions of the United States, that defies reality, and that produces dangerous action.

Does all this seem unrealistic? It should not; cascades often occur in the real world. The real estate boom of the early twenty-first century, culminating in the subprime crisis, was a product of a cascade.[134] When there are speculative bubbles, people are typically relying not on fundamentals but on their judgments about what other people are likely to think and do. Hence prices can continue to go up simply because people think that other people are investing—until a crash occurs. It was widely thought, and said, that real estate prices always go up, even though this is false. By historical standards since 1940, home prices jumped spectacularly only in one period: from 1997 to 2004. In that period, many people thought, and said, that it is in the nature of home prices to increase over time, and people's behavior tracked their belief. But the belief was demonstrably false. For many decades, home prices were relatively stable, until the unprecedented boom that began in 1997.

As Robert Shiller has shown, the best explanation of the real estate bubble greatly overlaps with the best explanation of the stock market bubble of the late 1990s: In both cases, people were greatly influenced by a process of social contagion that amounted to an informational cascade. This belief produced wildly unrealistic projections, with palpable consequences for home purchases and mortgage choices. In 2005, Shiller and Karl Case conducted a survey among San Francisco home buyers. The median expected price increase, over the next decade, was 9 percent per year! In fact, one-third of those surveyed thought that the annual increase would be much higher than that. Their baseless optimism was based on two factors: salient price increases in the recent past and the apparent, and contagious, optimism of other people.

Of course the stock of public knowledge depends not merely on word-of-mouth and on visible sales, but on the media as well. In the late 1990s and early 2000s, it was widely reported that home prices were rapidly increasing (true) and that the prices would continue to increase over time (not true). If the apparent experts confirm "what everyone knows," then seemingly risky deals, of the sort that have led so many people to disaster, will seem hard to resist. The Internet bubble of the late 1990s was a result of similar forces, producing its own form of extremism. Notwithstanding the underlying evidence about values, people believed that continued growth was highly likely, because of what other people thought (combined with recent events); terrible investment choices resulted.

Do cascades occur for cultural products, such as art, music, movies, and literature? They certainly do, and they can produce unpredictable extreme movements. For a fascinating example, consider a study of music downloads. Matthew Salganik and his coauthors[135] created an artificial music market, with 14,341 participants who were visitors to a Web site popular with young people. The participants were given a list of previously unknown songs from unknown bands. They were asked to listen to a brief selection of any songs that interested them, to decide which songs (if any) to download, and to assign a rating to the songs they chose. About half of the participants were asked to make their decisions independently, based on the names of the bands and the songs and their own judgment about the quality of the music. The other half could see how many times each song had been downloaded by other participants. These participants were also randomly assigned to one or another of eight possible "worlds," with each evolving on its own; those in any particular world could see only the downloads in their own world. The key question was whether people would be affected by the choices of others—and whether different music would become popular in the different "worlds."

Did cascades develop? Were there extreme movements? There is not the slightest doubt. In all eight worlds, individuals were far more likely to download songs that had been previously downloaded in significant numbers—and far less likely to download songs that had not been so popular. Most strikingly, the success of songs was quite unpredictable. The songs that did well or poorly in the control group, where people did not see other people's judgments, could perform very differently in the "social influence worlds." In those worlds, most songs could become very popular or very unpopular, with much depending on the choices of the first downloaders. The identical song could be a hit or a failure, simply because other people, at the start, were seen to choose to download it or not. As Salganik and his coauthors put it: "In general, the 'best' songs never do very badly, and the 'worst' songs never do extremely well," but (and this is the remarkable point) "almost any other result is possible."

As we have seen, similar findings have been made in the context of jury judgments about punitive damage awards. There is a great deal of unpredictability for identical cases, in part because social influences among jurors can spur juries to make extremely high awards. As with jury judgments, so, too, with music (and movies and books and political views): Because people pay attention to one another, an early movement in a particular direction can operate as a spark that ignites a fire, leading to unexpected and dramatic outcomes. Many domains have what economists call "multiple equilibria"—a range of possible outcomes, all stable, and all possible with modest differences in starting points. People are often tempted to think, after the fact, that an outcome was entirely predictable and that the success of a musician, an actor, an author, or a politician was inevitable in light of his or her skills and characteristics. Social influences suggest that we should beware of that temptation. Small interventions and even coincidences, at a key stage, can produce large variations in the ultimate outcome.

For a less entertaining example, consider the existence of widely divergent group judgments about the origins and causes of AIDS—with some groups believing, falsely, that the first cases were observed in Africa as a result of sexual relations between human beings and monkeys, and with other groups believing, also falsely, that the virus was produced in government laboratories.[136] These and other views about AIDS are a product of social interactions and, in particular, of cascade effects. Deliberation often fails, and extreme views often spread, as a result. When groups come to believe some alleged fact about the egregious misconduct of some person or nation, an informational cascade is often at work.

Reputational Cascades

In a reputational cascade, people think that they know what is right, or what is likely to be right, but they nonetheless go along with the crowd to maintain the good opinion of others. Suppose that Albert suggests that global warming will produce catastrophic harm in the near future and that Barbara concurs with Albert, not because she actually thinks that Albert is right, but because she does not wish to seem, to Albert, to be ignorant or indifferent to environmental protection. If Albert and Barbara say that global warming will produce catastrophic harm in the near future, Cynthia might not contradict them publicly and might even appear to share their judgment—not because she believes that judgment to be correct, but because she does not want to face their hostility or lose their good opinion.

It should be easy to see how this process might generate a cascade. Once Albert, Barbara, and Cynthia offer a united front on the issue, their friend David might be reluctant to contradict them, even if he thinks that they are wrong. The apparently shared view of Albert, Barbara, and Cynthia carries information; that view might be right. But even if David has reason to believe that they are wrong, he might not want to take them on publicly. The problem, of course, is that the group will not hear what David knows. Reputational cascades often help to account for the spread of extreme views. Especially when people live in some kind of enclave, they may silence themselves in the face of an emerging judgment or opinion, even if they believe it to be wrong.

In the actual world of group decisions, people are, of course, uncertain whether publicly expressed statements are a product of independent knowledge, participation in an informational cascade, or reputational pressure. Much of the time, listeners and observers overstate the extent to which the actions of others are based on independent information rather than social pressures. Deliberating groups often move to extreme points as a result.

Politics

There is every reason to think that cascade effects occur for issues of politics and morality—and that such effects can produce dramatic and extreme movements. Suppose that people are asking whether a politician would make a good nominee for high office. Informational cascades are highly likely; indeed, an informational cascade helped to account for the Democratic nominations of both John Kerry in 2004[137] and Barack Obama in 2008. When Democrats shifted from Howard Dean to John Kerry, or from Hillary Clinton to Barack Obama, it was not because each Democratic voter made an independent judgment on behalf of Kerry or Obama. It was in large part because of a widespread perception that other people were flocking to the eventual winner. With respect to Kerry, Duncan Watts's account is worth quoting at length, because it captures the general dynamic so well:

> A few weeks before the Iowa caucuses, Kerry's campaign seemed dead, but then he unexpectedly won Iowa, then New Hampshire, and then primary after primary. How did this happen? ... When everyone is looking to someone else for an opinion—trying, for example, to pick the Democratic candidate they think everyone else will pick—it's possible that whatever information other people might have gets lost, and instead we get a cascade of imitation that, like a stampeding herd, can start for no apparent reason and subsequently go in any direction with equal likelihood. Stock market bubbles and cultural fads are the examples that most people associate with cascades ... but the same dynamics can show up even in the serious business of Democratic primaries. ... We think of ourselves as autonomous individuals, each driven by our own internal abilities and desires and therefore solely responsible for our own behavior, particularly when it comes to voting. No voter ever admits—even to herself—that she chose Kerry because he won New Hampshire.

A similar process greatly benefited Obama, who focused on the Iowa primary at a time when he was trailing badly in the national polls. After he won that primary, both informational and reputational cascades developed on his behalf, propelling him to the nomination. Information about his qualities spread rapidly among people who had theretofore known nothing about him. Those who admired Obama and made favorable statements about him received reputational benefits; social pressures worked to his advantage.

Social cascades can be found for many contested political questions, including the legitimacy of same-sex marriage, abortion, particular wars, and capital punishment. Perspectives on both environmental and economic issues are often a product of cascade effects. Few of us have thought long and hard about these questions. We often end up thinking what we think others think—at least if we think that those others think like we do. When "political correctness" moves people dramatically to the left or to the right, cascades are typically involved. These points raise an additional warning flag about any situation in which citizens sort themselves into communities of like-minded others. In such communities, cascades are almost inevitable, and they might well be based on poor thinking and confusion. The problem is that the same forces that produce factual errors operate in the moral and political domains as well.

CHAPTER 3

Movements

An understanding of group polarization and cascade effects has implications for all sorts of social beliefs and movements. Let us now consider some examples. For any of them, of course, a whole volume would be necessary to give a full sense of the underlying dynamics. My goal here is not to provide that full sense, but to say enough to suggest that the social influences explored here have played a crucial role.

OPPOSITIONAL MOVEMENTS AND GEOGRAPHIC ISOLATION

Under what circumstances will a group of people, with some degree of commonality, form a shared sense not only of identity but also of grievance, and ultimately seek to oppose existing social practices? Why do oppositional movements occur?

The real world is messy; it is not a controlled experiment. But for a clue, consider Sharon Groch's discussion of the movement for disability rights. Groch focuses above all on deaf people, whose sense of shared identity was enhanced by a high degree of geographical isolation.[1] Among the group of disabled people, the deaf are the most mobilized, largely because they live, much of the time, in the same geographical spaces. By contrast, those with impaired mobility are far less mobilized, in part because they have not been segregated and have not formed a strong sense of collective identity. Blind people are an intermediate case. Because of early residential schools, blind people have occasionally developed a kind of an oppositional culture. But because they have often been integrated into public schools and otherwise lacked geographical isolation, the culture was weakly developed.

Groch's conclusion? Everything depends on whether disabled people have "free spaces, or spaces of autonomous action."[2] The ability is greatly affected by a group's physical segregation. With such segregation, groups of disabled people are more likely to have found free spaces, in which they are able to share concerns and to develop a sense that they stand in opposition to the rest of society. Groch's account fits exceedingly well with the findings I have emphasized. If a group has "free spaces," it has a degree of separation, and polarization might well occur, at least if group members start with a sense of grievance or a level of concern. By contrast, a group that is diffused within the general population and lacks "spaces of autonomous action" will have little opportunity for discussion limited to group members—and hence an oppositional consciousness, fueled by polarization, is far less likely to arise.

These points help to explain variations among disabled people and also cast light on the dynamics behind social movements involving race, gender, age, and sexual orientation. Some of those dynamics are most unfortunate from the standpoint of social justice. Among the class of disabled people, some of the strongest moral claims for social support can be made by those with mental illness, such as depression and obsessive-compulsive disorder. Mental illness can be crippling, often far more so than severe physical illness, in the sense that it severely undermines people's ability to enjoy their lives. A great deal might be, and should be, done to help those who are suffering. But the mentally ill do not have free spaces, and by the very nature of their illness, they are rarely able to organize and to ask for accommodation or assistance. With respect to race, gender, age, and sexual orientation, successful reform movements have often occurred simply because of processes of polarization, as people assembled into groups of the like-minded.[3] There is no question that movements for equality, on various grounds, involve group polarization.

BUBBLES, BAD INVESTMENTS, AND THE SUBPRIME CRISIS OF 2008

Many people believe that markets are "efficient" in the sense that they reflect widely dispersed information, and hence reveal more knowledge than any single person or board, however expert, is likely to have. Even if this claim is correct, it should be clear that small groups of investors, speaking with one another, may polarize in a way that produces large-scale mistakes. In an exceptionally illuminating discussion, Brooke Harrington has provided a great deal of supportive evidence.[4] "Investment clubs" are small groups of people who pool their money and make joint decisions about investments in the stock market. Harrington shows that the worst-performing clubs are primarily social, and their members listen closely to one another. They know each other, eat together, and are connected by bonds of affection. The low performers usually have unanimous votes, with little open debate. Their votes are cast to build social cohesion rather than to produce the highest returns. By contrast, the best-performing clubs offer limited social connections and are focused on increasing returns. Dissent is far more frequent in the high-performing clubs. In the low performers, social interactions produce both cascade effects and a high degree of polarization, to the great detriment of their members.

Unfortunately, these effects are not limited to members of investment clubs. Informational cascades play a large role in investments as a whole, and they sometimes produce bubbles, in a way that raises serious problems for the claimed efficiency of markets.[5] What accounts for the subprime crisis of 2008 and the eventual financial crisis for the United States as a whole? A full answer would require many pages. But as I have suggested, part of the picture is a shared social belief that real estate prices always go up, so that apparently risky investments and mortgages were inevitably a good idea. The claim of ever-increasing prices created a classic bubble. People believed that prices would go up because other people believed that prices would go up, and this widely held belief led companies and individuals to make a series of decisions that would ultimately produce disaster.

The best account has been given by Robert Shiller, who emphasizes that "the most important single element to be reckoned with in understanding this or any other speculative boom is the *social contagion* of boom thinking, mediated by the common observation of rapidly rising prices."[6] Shiller says that social contagion operates like a disease epidemic, in the sense that both have an infection rate, which involves spreading, and a removal rate, which involves recovery or death. When an optimistic view of the market prevails, it is because the infection rate is higher than the removal rate.

Eventually, public knowledge is subject to a kind of escalation or spiral, in which everyone seems to think that the
optimistic view is correct. As the media endorses that view,
people come to believe that we are in a "new era," and
feedback loops help to bring about ever-increasing prices.
"The price-story-price loop repeats again and again during a
speculative bubble."[7]

Shiller explicitly suggests that on this account, speculative bubbles are produced by informational cascades, as
people suppress their own doubts in light of what everyone
else appears to think. Group polarization is at work as well,
leading people to greater confidence in a relatively extreme
belief. What happened with the real estate boom is not
radically different from what happened with respect to
political issues in our Colorado experiment (see chapter 1).

Of course, it is always possible to give such an account in
hindsight, but some people, above all Shiller, predicted it
well in advance and with explicit reference to the effects of
social interactions and cascade effects in producing the real
estate bubble.[8] Shiller finds it "clear" that an informational
"cascade helped to create the housing bubble. And it is now
possible that a downward cascade will develop—in which
rational individuals become excessively pessimistic as they
see others bidding down home prices to abnormally low
levels."[9]

ETHNIC MOVEMENTS AND "ETHNIFICATION"

When ethnic conflict breaks out, it is tempting to think that
primordial hatreds have bubbled up to the surface. On this
view, ethnic hatred arises as long-suppressed ethnic and
religious antagonisms come into full bloom. All over the
world, ethnic conflict might be seen as a flowering of buried
resentments and angers.

But there is a real problem with this view, which is that ethnic hatreds are not in any sense primordial. They are not in anyone's blood. They are often a product of a kind of rapid "ethnification," spurred by group polarization. Many people who participate in ethnic strife and show intense ethnic antagonism are influenced decisively by recent social pressures, not by anything from the distant past. Indeed, governments themselves can work hard to inculcate and to maintain cross-border hostilities. When they are born, North Koreans have nothing against the Japanese. But the government of North Korea has tried to portray the nation's history in a way that suggests that the people of Japan, present as well as past, are enemies. The hostility expressed against the Japanese by many people in North Korea is emphatically a product of current pressures.

More generally, levels of ethnic activity vary greatly over time and space. In most American cities, for example, most people do not act publicly in a way that draws even the slightest attention to their ethnicity. (I put ethnic parades, such as St. Patrick's Day, to one side.) Most of the time, clothing, hairstyles, and the like do not differ significantly across religious, ethnic, and racial lines. Asian Americans do not dress differently from whites, and it is usually not possible to tell, from clothing and hairstyles, whether someone is Catholic, Jewish, Episcopalian, Buddhist, or atheist. The absence of distinctions on multiple grounds should be contrasted with domains in which clothing and hairstyles do indeed differ; consider the fairly sharp differences between men and women, young and old, and rich and poor.

Indeed, each of these cases has its own distinctive interest, with modest or extreme differences, from one period to another, between men and women, young and old, or rich and poor. With respect to class, Gordon Wood's account of social differences in America before the Revolution makes the point. In that period, American society was extremely hierarchical, and with respect to dress and manners, "common people" were "made to recognize and feel their inferiority and subordination to gentlemen. ... But since their ignorance, inferiority, and subordination seemed part of the natural order of things, many common folk ... dutifully made their bows and doffed their caps before ladies and gentlemen; they knew their place and willingly walked while gentlefolk rode; and as yet they seldom expressed any burning desire to change place with their betters."[10]

Many societies have shown slow or rapid increases in ethnification, as people devote more of their efforts to showcasing their ethnic identity. Relevant clothing, hairstyles, or dialects grow in use over time. We can easily find eras in the United States in which ethnic identification grew (usually just a bit) or declined (sometimes a lot).[11] As Hitler obtained power, many German Jews became more closely self-identified as Jewish, in part for reasons of self-protection. Many others masked their religion, also for reasons of self-protection. Ethnification and its opposite were concrete responses to the Nazi threat. We can generalize from this example: When an ethnic or religious group is at risk, its members might bind together and stress what unifies them or might instead attempt to assimilate. Much of the time, their decisions will reflect some kind of assessment of what strategy is likely to provide the most protection.

Return to differences of gender, age, and wealth, where clothing and hairstyle differences are pervasive. Social pressures punish women who dress like men, or old people who dress like young people, or rich people who dress like poor people. (Men who dress like women are subject to special punishment.) The relevant differences are intensified by such pressures. And in some times and places, the pressures are reduced or even switch direction—as, for example, when men and women are encouraged to dress alike (mostly, to be sure, as men traditionally do).

Consider the question of ethnification in this light. A key question here is whether the relevant social norms impose pressure to identify in ethnic terms, or not to do so. It may be "politically correct" to broadcast one's ethnicity, or it may be politically correct to hide it. Sometimes the governing norms differ from one location to another. Sometimes they shift abruptly. When this is so, there can be intense pressure to self-identify in ethnic terms, sometimes to retain friends, sometimes to obtain material advantages, sometimes to save one's life. "Identity entrepreneurs" of various kinds can increase the pressure to emphasize ethnicity. It follows that ethnic identifications may well be a product of contemporary pressure and have little or nothing to do with anything ancient or primordial. And when ethnic identifications occur, group polarization, or a kind of ethnic cascade, may well be at work.

With a focus on ethnic hatreds in the former Yugoslavia, the underlying processes have been illuminatingly discussed by economist Timur Kuran.[12] Kuran's central claim is that a reputational cascade helps to explain the rise of ethnification. Kuran shows that even at a late stage, people in the former Yugoslavia lived together harmoniously across ethnic lines. Indeed, those lines were essentially irrelevant. Supposedly primordial hatreds played no role in the lives of most people. Old historical events were hardly salient. Indeed, they were barely known, and often entirely unknown. But as Kuran writes:

> Within months, millions of Serbs who had shown little ethnic fervor began paying attention to ethnic statistics, promoting symbols of Serb exclusiveness, vilifying and ostracizing non-Serbs, referring frequently to the sufferings of their ancestors, and supporting the enlargement of Serbian-held territories ... Previously happy

mixed marriages disintegrated. Historical events that had mattered not at all suddenly became central to political debates.[13]

The major conclusion is that even the most intense forms of ethnic hatred and fear can be a *product* of a process of ethnification, rather than a *cause* of that process. A careful investigation of any particular situation is necessary, of course, to know whether this conclusion holds for that situation. But recall that ethnic hatred is not in anyone's blood. Whether people focus on ethnic identity or on something else is largely a product of (current and recent) social pressures—emphatically including group polarization—not of anything that happened in the distant past. This point strongly suggests the possibility of multiple equilibria: With relatively small shocks, a population that did not much separate along ethnic lines might come to do so.

While these issues are relevant to nations once suffering from ethnic conflict, ethnification can occur in any nation, even those lacking ethnic violence. We can find close analogues whenever people come to identify more closely along particular demographic lines, involving such characteristics as gender, political conviction, age, disability, or sexual orientation. What is particularly interesting is how and when it becomes desirable to identify, or to refuse to identify, in such terms, as mounting social pressures suggest that people ought to do one or the other. And here, too, a key point is that with seemingly small differences, at one or another stage, social outcomes might turn out to be radically different from what they would otherwise be.

CONSPIRACY THEORIES

Why do people accept conspiracy theories that turn out to be false and for which the evidence is weak or even nonexistent?[14] It is tempting to answer in terms of individual pathology.[15] Perhaps conspiracy theories are a product of mental illness, such as paranoia or narcissism. And indeed, some people who accept conspiracy theories are mentally ill and subject to delusions. But in many communities and even nations, such theories are widely held. It is not plausible to suggest that all or most members of those communities are afflicted by mental illness. The most important conspiracy theories are hardly limited to those who suffer from any kind of pathology.

For present purposes, the most useful way to understand the pervasiveness of conspiracy theories is to examine how people acquire their beliefs. For most of what they believe they know, human beings lack personal or direct information; they must rely on what other people think. We have seen that in some domains, people suffer from a "crippled epistemology," in the sense that they know very few things, and what they know is wrong.[16] Many extremists fall in this category; their extremism stems not from irrationality but from the fact that they have little (relevant) information, and their extremist views are supported by what little they know.[17] Conspiracy theorizing often has the same feature. Those who believe that Israel was responsible for the attacks of 9/11 or that the Central Intelligence Agency killed President Kennedy may well be responding quite rationally to the informational signals they receive.

Consider here the suggestive claim that terrorism is more likely to arise in nations that lack civil rights and civil liberties.[18] If this is so, it might be because terrorism is not abstract violence but an extreme form of political protest, and when people lack the usual outlets for registering their protest, they might resort to violence.[19] But consider another possibility: When civil rights and civil liberties are restricted, little information is available, and what comes from government cannot be trusted. If the most trustworthy or least untrustworthy information justifies conspiracy theories and (therefore) extremism and (therefore?) violence, then terrorism is more likely to arise.

Of course, it is necessary to specify how, exactly, conspiracy theories begin. Some such theories seem to bubble up spontaneously, appearing roughly simultaneously in many different social networks; others are initiated and spread, quite intentionally, by *conspiracy entrepreneurs* who profit directly or indirectly from propagating their theories. One example is the French author Thierry Meyssan, whose book *9/11: The Big Lie* became a best seller and a sensation for its claims that the Pentagon explosion on 9/11 was caused by a missile, fired as the opening salvo of a coup d'état by the military-industrial complex, rather than by American Airlines Flight 77. (In the context of the 9/11 attacks, there are many other examples.[20]) Some conspiracy entrepreneurs are entirely sincere; others are interested in money or power or in achieving some general social goal. In the context of the AIDS virus, a diverse set of people initiated rumors, many involving conspiracies, and in view of the confusion and fear surrounding that virus, several of those rumors spread widely.[21] But even for conspiracy theories put about by conspiracy entrepreneurs, the key question is why some theories take hold while many more do not, and vanish into obscurity.

Whenever a bad event has occurred, rumors and speculation are inevitable. Most people are not able to know, on the basis of personal or direct knowledge, why an airplane crashed, why a leader was assassinated, or why a terrorist attack succeeded. In the aftermath of such an event, numerous speculations will be offered, and some of them are likely to point to some kind of conspiracy. To some people, those speculations will seem plausible, perhaps because they provide a suitable outlet for outrage and blame, perhaps because the speculation fits well with other deeply rooted beliefs they hold. Terrible events produce outrage, and when people are outraged, they are all the more likely to seek causes that justify their emotional states and also to attribute those events to intentional action.[22] Conspiracy theories, like rumors, may simultaneously relieve strong emotions and offer an explanation (to those who accept the theory) of why they feel as they do; the theory relieves those emotions at the same time that it rationalizes.

In addition, antecedent beliefs are a key to the success or failure of conspiracy theories. Some people would find it impossibly jarring to think that the CIA was responsible for the assassination of a civil rights leader; that thought would unsettle too many of their other judgments. Others would find those other judgments strongly supported, even confirmed, by the suggestion that the CIA was responsible for such an assassination. Compare the case of terrorist attacks. For most Americans, a claim that the U.S. government attacked its own citizens, for some ancillary purpose, would make it impossible to hold onto a wide range of other judgments. Clearly this point does not hold for many people in Islamic nations, for whom it is far from jarring to believe that responsibility lies with the United States (or Israel).

In short, people are motivated to accept accounts that fit with their preexisting convictions; acceptance of those accounts makes them feel better, and acceptance of competing accounts makes them feel worse.[23] Reactions to a claim of conspiracy to assassinate a political leader, or to commit or allow some atrocity either domestically or abroad, are often determined by the motivations of those who hear the claim. People also have good reasons to accept accounts that fit with what they already know; if a conspiracy theory is deeply jarring in light of your existing knowledge, then you have a good reason to reject it. Here, as elsewhere, people attempt to find some kind of equilibrium among their assortment of beliefs, and acceptance or rejection of a conspiracy theory will often depend on which of the two leads to equilibrium.

These are points about individual judgments, bracketing social influences. But after some bad event has occurred, those influences are crucial, for most people will have little or no direct information about what caused the event. How many people know, directly or on the basis of personal investigation, whether Al Qaeda was responsible for the 9/11 attacks, whether Lee Harvey Oswald killed President Kennedy on his own, or whether a tragic death in an apparent airplane accident was truly accidental? Inevitably, people must rely on the beliefs of other people. Some people will require a great deal of evidence to accept a conspiracy theory; others will require much less. People will therefore have different thresholds for accepting or rejecting such a theory and for acting on the basis of the theory.[24] One way to meet a relevant threshold is to supply direct or indirect evidence. Another way is simply to show that some, many, or most (trusted) people accept or reject the theory. These are the appropriate circumstances for social cascades—in particular, informational cascades—whose dynamics, while not unique to conspiracy theories, help to explain how they spread.

Informational cascades can occur without any particular triggering event. But a distinctive kind of cascade arises when such an event is highly salient or cognitively "available." In the context of many risks, such as those associated with terrorism, nuclear power, and abandoned hazardous waste dumps, a particular event initiates a cascade, and it stands as a trigger or a symbol justifying public concern, regardless of whether that concern is warranted.[25] Availability cascades occur through the interaction between a salient event and social influences, both informational and reputational. Often political actors, both self-interested and altruistic, work hard to produce such cascades.

Conspiracy theories are driven by the same mechanisms. A particular event becomes available, and conspiracy theories are invoked, both in explaining it and in using it as a symbol for broader social forces, casting doubt on accepted wisdom in many domains. Within certain nations and groups, the claim that the United States or Israel was responsible for the attacks of 9/11 fits well within a general narrative about who is the aggressor and who is the liar in a series of disputes—and the view that Al Qaeda was responsible raises questions about that same narrative. Conspiracy theories are frequently a product of availability cascades.

Thus far, the account has been purely cognitive: Conspiracy theories circulate in the same way that other beliefs circulate, as people give weight to the views of others and attend to their own reputations. But it is clear that affective factors, and not mere information, play a large role in the circulation of rumors of all kinds, including conspiracy theories. Many rumors persist and spread because they serve to justify or rationalize an antecedent emotional state produced by some important event, such as a disaster or a war. When people are especially angry or fearful, they may be more likely to focus on particular sorts of rumors and to spread them to others. And when rumors trigger intense feelings, they are far more likely to be circulated.

Experimental evidence strongly supports this speculation in the analogous context of urban legends.[26] When urban legends—involving, for example, a decapitated motorcycle rider, a rat in a soda bottle, or cat food mislabeled as tuna—are devised so as to trigger strong emotions (such as disgust), people are more likely to pass them along. Perhaps the most revealing of these experiments involved the actual spreading of urban legends on the Internet.[27] The conclusion is that in the marketplace of ideas, "emotional selection" plays a significant role, and it helps to explain such diverse phenomena as moral panics about deviant behavior, hysteria about child abuse, and media attention to relatively small sources of risk such as road rage and "flesh-eating bacteria."[28] A particular problem involves "emotional snowballing"—runaway selection for emotional content rather than for information.[29]

The application to conspiracy theories should not be obscure. When a terrible event has occurred, acceptance of such theories may justify or rationalize the affective state produced by that event; consider conspiracy theories in response to political assassinations. In addition, such theories typically involve accounts, or rumors, that create intense emotions, such as indignation, thus producing a kind of emotional selection that will spread beliefs from one person to another. Of course, evidence matters. So long as there is some kind of process for meeting falsehoods with truth, mistaken beliefs can be corrected. But sometimes the conditions for correction are not present.

For purposes of understanding the spread of conspiracy theories, it is especially important to note that group polarization is particularly likely, and particularly pronounced, when people have a shared sense of identity and are connected by bonds of solidarity. These are circumstances in which arguments by outsiders, unconnected with the group, will lack much credibility and fail to have much of an effect in reducing polarization.

A crippled epistemology can arise not only from informational and reputational dynamics within a given group but also from self-selection of members into and out of groups with extreme views. Once polarization occurs or cascades arise, and the group's median view begins to move in a certain direction, doubters and halfway believers will tend to depart, while intense believers remain. The overall size of the group may shrink, but the group may also pick up new believers who are even more committed, and in any event, the remaining members will, by self-selection, display more fanaticism. Group members may engage in a kind of doublethink, segregating themselves, in a physical or informational sense, to protect their beliefs from challenge by outsiders.[30] As a result, group polarization will intensify.

OUTRAGE, SOCIAL INFLUENCES, AND TERRORISM

We have seen that punishment judgments are rooted in outrage; a kind of "outrage heuristic" has a strong effect on those judgments.[31] Hence a group's outrage on a bounded scale is an excellent predictor of the same group's punishment judgments on the same scale.[32] We have seen that people who begin with a high level of outrage become still more outraged as a result of group discussion. Moreover, the degree of the shift depends on the level of outrage before people start to talk. The higher the original level of outrage, the greater the shift as a result of internal deliberations.[33]

There is a point here about the social dynamics behind not only severe punishment by jurors, mobs, and governments but also rebellion and violence. Outrage accounts for these as well. If like-minded people, predisposed to be outraged, are put together, significant changes are to be expected. It should be easy to see that group polarization, intensifying outrage, is inevitably at work in feuds, international strife, and war. One of the characteristic features of feuds is that members of feuding groups tend to talk to only one another, or at least listen only to one another, fueling and amplifying their outrage, while solidifying their impression of the relevant events.

In this light, some notes on the topic of terrorism will be useful, partly because it is of independent interest, and partly because the processes involved in terrorism can find analogues in far more benign processes. When groups become caught up in misunderstanding, suspicion, hatred, or violence, it is often a product of the social mechanisms discussed here.

It is tempting to think that terrorism is a product of extreme poverty, lack of education, or a kind of mental illness. It turns out that all of these thoughts are quite wrong.[34] Terrorists are usually not poor, and they generally do not grow up in economic distress. Most of the time, they come from middle-income families. Nor have terrorists lacked education.[35] There is no evidence that they suffer from mental illness. We have seen that if for the goal is to identify social practices that are associated with terrorism, a lack of civil rights and civil liberties seems to provide a clue. Alan Krueger argues that terrorism is a form of political protest, and those who lack civil rights and civil liberties, not having other means of engaging in protest, resort to terrorism.[36] To Krueger's point, we might add that when civil liberties do not exist, citizens have in essence only one prominent source of information—the state—and that source cannot be trusted. If dissidents or opponents of the regime succeed in spreading information, what they say might well be credible, if only because official sources cannot credibly combat it. In addition, nations that suppress civil rights and civil liberties deserve, and are often seen to deserve, widespread opposition on the part of their citizens. These are promising circumstances for the rise of terrorism.

The key point is that authoritarian nations produce a crippled epistemology on the part of their citizens. When those interested in violent acts offer accounts of what is happening and what must be done, they are peculiarly likely to find fertile ground. In a democracy, by contrast, the existence of ample information, with some kind of market-place of ideas, is more likely to defang terrorists, simply because their accounts can be shown to be implausible. I am not suggesting that terrorism cannot or does not occur in free societies; it can and it does. I am suggesting only that other things being equal, the likelihood of terror-ism is reduced, not only because political protest can be expressed in other ways but also because terrorism is likely to have less appeal.

All the evidence suggests that terrorism is a product of social networks, in which those inclined to violence work hard to recruit others.[37] Terrorist leaders act as polarization entrepreneurs. They help to create enclaves of like-minded people. They stifle dissenting views and do not tolerate internal disagreement. They take steps to ensure a high degree of internal solidarity. They restrict the relevant argu-ment pool and take full advantage of reputational forces, above all by using the incentives of group approval and disapproval. Terrorist acts themselves are motivated by these forces and incentives. In fact, terrorist organizations impose psychological pressures to accelerate the movement in extreme directions. Here group membership plays a key role. Thus:

> Another result of psychological motivation is the intensity of group dynamics among terrorists. They tend to demand unanimity and be intolerant of dissent. With the enemy clearly identified and un-equivocally evil, pressure to escalate the frequency and intensity of operations is ever present. The need to belong to the group

discourages resignations, and the fear of compromise disallows their acceptance. Compromise is rejected, and terrorist groups lean toward maximalist positions. . . . In societies in which people identify themselves in terms of group membership (family, clan, tribe), there may be a willingness to self-sacrifice seldom seen elsewhere.[38]

Training routines specifically reinforce the basic message of solidarity amid outrage and humiliation. Terrorists have many predecessors here. Adolf Hitler similarly attempted to create group membership and fuel movements toward extremes, by stressing the suffering and the humiliation of the German people. This is a characteristic strategy of warmongers and terrorists of all stripes, for humiliation fuels outrage. "Many al-Qaida trainees saw videos . . . daily as part of their training routine. Showing hundreds of hours of Muslims in dire straits—Palestinians . . . Bosnians . . . Chechens . . . Iraqi children—[was] all part of al-Qaida's induction strategy."[39]

In the particular context of Al Qaeda, there has been a pervasive effort to link Muslims all over the globe, above all by emphasizing a shared identity, one that includes a victimized "us" and excludes an oppressive "them." Thus Osama bin Laden "appeals to a pervasive sense of humiliation and powerlessness in Islamic countries. Muslims are victims the world over . . . Bosnia, Somalia, Palestine, Chechnya, and . . . Saudi Arabia. . . . [H]e makes the world simple for people who are otherwise confused, and gives them a sense of mission."[40] Hence there are unmistakable cultlike features to the indoctrination effort: "[T]he military training [in Al Qaeda camps] is accompanied by forceful religious indoctrination, with recruits being fed a stream of anti-western propaganda and being incessantly reminded about their duty to perform jihad."[41] Intense connections are built into the very structure of these efforts. "The structure of Al Qaeda, an all-male enterprise . . . appears to involve small groups of relatively young men who maintain strong bonds with each other, bonds whose intensity is dramatised and heightened by the secrecy demanded by their missions and the danger of their projects."[42]

In recent years, terrorism has been produced less by leaders than by a more spontaneous process, in which small networks of people help to produce radicalization. Thus "Al Qaeda Central" must be distinguished from a much more loosely organized Al Qaeda social movement. In the words of Marc Sageman, the "global Islamic terrorist social movement forms through the spontaneous self-organization of informal 'bunches of guys,' trusted friends, from the bottom up."[43] An initial clue: A strong majority of people in Sageman's sample were expatriates, and they joined a terrorist organization while residing in a nation in which they did not grow up. Indeed, four-fifths of his sample included people who were either expatriates or sons or grandsons of Muslim immigrants to the West. They joined the global Islamist terrorist social movement as a result of either friendship or kinship. Coming to the West as young adults, many of them searched for and found childhood friends in their new country and became involved in terrorism as a result. Many others joined relatives who were already part of the terrorist movement. Still others consisted of "a 'bunch of guys' who collectively decided to join a terrorist organization."[44]

To a considerable extent, Islamic terrorism has been spurred by the spontaneous self-organization of informal collections of people. In most cases, the ideological commitment was predated by social bonds: friendship and family first, political extremism second. Sageman registers his own surprise at "the lack of top-down recruitment program into Al Qaeda. There was no campaign drive for new members, no dedicated committee for recruitment, and no budget allocated specifically for this task."

Terrorism often results from a process of radicalization, which starts with a degree of moral outrage. Many eventual terrorists see, on the Internet or on television, greatly disturbing events and images, such as the killing of Muslim children. For some people, the resulting sense of outrage becomes part of a broader narrative in which "wannabe terrorists" come to understand themselves as engaged in a kind of war against those who are plotting against people like them. That narrative will not, of course, make sense to everyone. It must also resonate with personal experiences. For many Muslim expatriates in Europe, those experiences include exclusion and discrimination. Expatriates and second-generation Muslims "compare themselves to their host peers. In Europe, they do not fare as well as the host young men. ... They interpret their perceived discrimination in the context of moral violations against Muslims elsewhere, and the notion that their local grievances are part of a more general hostility against Islam appears more compelling to them."[45]

In Sageman's account, a willingness to commit violent acts emerges as a result of social networks of two different kinds: face-to-face groups and virtual online groups. The former include radical mosques and radical Muslim student organizations, consisting largely of people who came to the West to study. These relatively informal groups exercise a major influence. In the extreme cases, they create a sense of a collective identity, whose members "start living in their own world." The resulting interactions show an acute form of group polarization, spawning a process of "in-group love," and ensure that "the group acts as an interactive 'echo chamber,' encouraging escalation of grievances and beliefs in conspiracy to the point of hatred."[46] Group members are not exactly irrational; instead, their sources of knowledge become sharply limited. They come to rely exclusively on one another to validate new information, and everything they believe is a product of interactions within their enclaves. Thus information refuting their beliefs is discarded as propaganda from the West.

To be sure, some group members reject the process of radicalization. They leave, ensuring a situation of voluntary sorting and self-selection in which only the true believers remain. Those believers regard themselves as close friends and even a substitute family. For them, it is especially difficult to depart.

Until 2004, face-to-face interactions played the key role in producing terrorist networks. More recently, the Internet has assumed great importance. Chat rooms and dedicated forums help to inspire many young Muslims to join the Islamic terrorist movement. As Sageman describes it, the role of the Internet has been unplanned, unruly, and dangerous. As police began to monitor physical meeting spaces, especially in Europe, like-minded young people started to exchange views and information online. Sageman's particular emphasis here is on active rather than passive users. Web sites, as such, are far less relevant than blogs and chat rooms, in which echo chambers help to radicalize people online. "The new forums have the same influence that these radical mosques played in the previous generation of terrorists." Conspiracy theories, fueling outrage, are spread in rapid fashion, as "individuals seek and select the rooms most compatible with their views and abandon the ones they disagree with. In a sense, the followers vote with their mice and select the views they like."

In short, interaction among like-minded people produces group polarization, with violent results. Sageman's account is worth quoting at some length:

> The other side of the coin of in-group love is out-group hate. Of course, this discrimination against the out-group is natural, but in

this case, it turns to hate through the group dynamics blending moral outrage, personal experience of discrimination and economic exclusion, and a specific interpretation tying everything together in a dangerous mix. Here, the group acts as an interactive "echo chamber," encouraging escalation of grievances and beliefs in conspiracy to the point of hatred. ... They disregard information refuting their beliefs as propaganda from the West. This progress is progressive. Those who believe that the group has gone too far in their growing radicalization peel off through the process of self-selection. Only the true believers remain.[47]

The simplest and most important point is that just as in the case of intense ethnic identification, terrorists are made, not born. More particularly, terrorists are made through identifiable social processes, emphatically involving group polarization. The most important lesson for law and policy is that if a nation aims to prevent terrorist activities, a good strategy is to prevent the rise of enclaves of like-minded people. Many of those who become involved in terrorist activities could end up doing something else with their lives. If the relevant associations are disrupted, terrorism will be far less likely to arise.

RATIONAL EXTREMISM?

Are extremists rational? We have seen that radicals often have a crippled epistemology,[48] in the sense that they know very little, and what they know supports what they think. "Isolation of people in a group with relatively limited contact with the larger society generates paranoid cognition, in which individuals begin to suppose the worst from those they do not know or even from those with whom they are not immediately in communication."[49] Paranoia is a mental illness, but in the context of most forms of extremism, the word should not be taken literally. As we have also seen, extremists do not usually suffer from mental illness. They think and act in accordance with what they have learned. In this sense, there is nothing irrational about extremism, at least from the standpoint of the individuals who have developed extremist beliefs.

Group polarization is a product, in large part, of the exchange of information. To be sure, those who polarize frequently assume that their own group is not skewed or biased; they fail to make proper adjustments for the motivations and limited information of group members.[50] But it is not easy to describe this failure as a form of irrationality.

What about the actions of extremists? To assess them, we need to know what extremists want, and we need to ask whether their actions are a good means of accomplishing their goals. In some influential writing, Robert Pape has suggested that suicide terrorism has a kind of "strategic logic."[51] Pape's claim is that suicide bombers have a specific goal, which is to force liberal democracies to make territorial concessions. In his view, the leadership groups that coordinate and direct suicide attacks are far from irrational. Most suicide attacks "are not isolated or random acts by individual fanatics but, rather, occur in clusters as part of a larger campaign by an organized political group to achieve a specific political goal."[52] That goal has typically been to coerce nations to withdraw from what the terrorists believe to be their national homeland. Increases in suicide terrorism have not been a product of undirected anger; the bombing has often worked, and hence there is more of it. Suicide attacks have helped persuade the Sri Lankan government to create an independent Tamil state, Israeli forces to leave Lebanon in 1985, American and French forces to leave Lebanon in 1983, and Israeli forces to leave the Gaza Strip and the West Bank in 1994 and 1995.[53]

Pape's own claims are controversial, and the class of extremists is far broader than the class of suicide bombers. To know whether terrorists are acting rationally, we need to specify their goals and to see if their methods are reasonably related to those goals. Often terrorists and extremists make big mistakes; some of their actions are self-defeating, producing deaths of their own members with little or no return, or even with a negative return. When like-minded types go to extremes, they may blunder badly by their own lights— as, for example, by making terrible investments,[54] by making bad strategic choices about war and peace,[55] or by erring on simple questions of fact. Pape is concerned with whether suicide bombers are choosing good means to their own ends. For terrorists, a key problem often involves their (hateful) ends, and it remains true that some of their means are ludicrously ineffective.

Nonetheless, it is true, and has been shown, that some extremists, including some terrorists, do choose sensible methods for accomplishing their goals. For those who want to reduce terrorism, a special problem is that those goals are frequently *indivisible*.[56] Extremists want control of land, or expulsion of outsiders, or establishment of a certain kind of society (e.g., a thoroughly Islamic one). Those who might be willing to bargain with them lack ways of dividing those goals into parts so as to permit stable accommodations. Polarization helps to establish those goals and to convince people to share them, but some extremists make shrewd decisions about how to get what they want. To that extent, they are hardly irrational, even when they are deadly.

But there are two wrinkles here. First, human beings often suffer from unrealistic optimism,[57] and extremists appear especially prone to that problem. About 90 percent of drivers believe that they are safer than the average driver and less likely to be involved in a serious accident.[58] Those who make war are often subject to unrealistic optimism as well.[59] It is reasonable to suggest that extremists, and in particular terrorists, have a greatly inflated sense of their own prospects for success. Second (and as we have seen), human beings use the "availability heuristic,"[60] which means that they assess probabilities by asking whether examples readily come to mind. Whether people will buy insurance for natural disasters is greatly affected by recent experiences.[61] People show "availability bias" when recent events make them inflate probabilities, and "unavailability bias" when the absence of recent events makes them deflate probabilities. Terrorists appear to fasten on actual or apparent successes, giving them an unjustified sense that violent actions are especially likely to succeed.

It should be clear that unrealistic optimism and availability bias can be a disastrous combination from the standpoint of both terrorists and their victims. Terrorists often make palpable errors, even from the standpoint of what they care about. But the larger point is that extremists are usually trying to find the best possible means of achieving their ends. No attempt to understand extremists or to prevent their actions can succeed if it treats them as "irrational."

This chapter has covered some large topics in a short space, and it will be helpful to summarize the key points. When groups go to extremes, it is usually because like-minded people have been able to congregate, often moving from an initial sense of concern to outrage, and eventually to action. Sometimes polarization uncovers a suppressed set of beliefs and desires, and sometimes it creates those very beliefs and desires. In the context of movements for rights, the beliefs and desires are usually there to begin with. And when people are seeking their rights, group polarization can be highly desirable. It helped the abolitionist movement in the United States. It also helped lead to the downfall of both apartheid and communism. The case of disability is especially illuminating, because the broad category includes diverse groups—for example, the blind, the deaf, the wheelchair-bound, the cognitively impaired, and the mentally ill. Disability rights movements have been a significant force for some of these groups but not for others, and social dynamics help to explain why.

Human beings are different from one another in countless ways, and when some differences are accentuated, it is usually because of group polarization. When ethnicity becomes highly salient, reputational pressures play a large role, and when ethnically connected people associate with one another and punish those who do not, the conditions for ethnification are in place. The key point here is that in many nations— including Iraq and the former Yugoslavia—many observers appeared to think that ancient hatreds, rather than new pressures, were the operative force. Since almost no one was alive during the events that produced those ancient hatreds, and since hatred is not in anyone's DNA, these observers were quite wrong. Ethnic identifications are not so unlike other cultural "products," such as music, literature, and movies. With some kind of nudge or push, things can become radically different from what they would otherwise be.

Whether terrorism is carefully orchestrated by leaders or more spontaneous, the perpetrators are typically not poor, not badly educated, not mentally ill, and not traumatized. Their conduct is a product of social networks and group polarization. There is a large lesson here not only for terrorism but also for crimes and outrageous actions of all kinds. As we will see, the lesson offers some valuable clues about what might be done by way of prevention.

CHAPTER 4

Preventing Extremism

Suppose that a nation seeks to prevent (unjustified) extremism. What might it do? I consider three possible answers here. The first, favored by many conservatives, is *traditionalism*. The second involves *consequentialism*. The third, prominent in the American founding, involves *checks and balances*; a system of freedom of expression and a diversity of views are part and parcel of that idea. We can associate these three responses with three people: Edmund Burke, Jeremy Bentham, and James Madison. I devote the most attention here to checks and balances, because that approach seems most interesting and most productive both in ordinary life and in the political domain.

TRADITIONALISM

For those who are concerned about extremism, it is natural to focus on Burke's great essay on the French Revolution, which can be understood as a sustained warning about the very processes I am exploring here. With his emphasis on the need to attend to traditions, Burke displayed a keen interest in popular passions and the risk that a group of people, stirred up by each other and one or another idea, can go in extreme directions.

Burke's central claim is that the "science of constructing a commonwealth, or reforming it, is, like every other experimental science, not to be taught a priori."[1] To make this argument, Burke opposes theories and abstractions, developed by individual minds, to traditions, built up by many minds over long periods. In his most vivid passage, Burke writes:

> We wished at the period of the Revolution, and do now wish, to derive all we possess as an inheritance from our forefathers. . . . The science of government being therefore so practical in itself, and intended for such practical purposes, a matter which requires experience, and even more experience than any person can gain in his whole life, however sagacious and observing he may be, it is with infinite caution than any man ought to venture upon pulling down an edifice which has answered in any tolerable degree, for ages the common purposes of society, or on building it up again, without having models and patterns of approved utility before his eyes.[2]

Thus Burke stresses the need to rely on experience and, in particular, the experience of generations. He objects to "pulling down an edifice," a metaphor capturing the objection to passionate movements that start social or political life from the ground up. It is for this reason that Burke describes the "spirit of innovation" as "the result of a selfish temper and confined views."[3] It is for the same reason that Burke offers the term "prejudice" as one of enthusiastic approval, noting that "instead of casting away all our old prejudices, we cherish them to a very considerable degree."[4]

Why, exactly, would prejudices appeal to Burke? The word itself supplies an answer. Prejudices operate before judgment—they supply answers that antedate reflection, including those forms of reflection that can be found and spread among group members. If prejudices are rooted in long-standing practices, it should not be surprising to find that Burke trusts them. Emphasizing the critical importance of stability, Burke adds a reference to "the evils of inconstancy and versatility, ten thousand times worse than those of obstinacy and the blindest prejudice."[5]

Burke's basic claim, then, is that reasonable citizens, aware of their own limitations, will effectively delegate a good deal of authority to their own traditions. "We are afraid to put men to live and trade each on his own private stock of reason" because of the concern that any one person's stock "is small, and that the individuals would do better to avail themselves of the general bank and capital of nations, and of ages. Many of our men of speculation, instead of exploding general prejudices, employ their sagacity to discover the latent wisdom which prevails in them."[6]

Traditionalism can certainly operate as a check on extreme movements. If group members have respect for what has been done before, they are unlikely to reject it in favor of what emerges from internal discussions. Those who respect traditions are most unlikely to polarize. But as a full response to the problems I have sketched here, traditionalism runs into serious difficulties. Traditions may persist not because they are good, but because of the same sorts of social influences that produce group polarization. After all, traditions convey information, and people may follow them not because they believe, independently, that they are good, but because other people (appear to have) believed that they are good. Thus people may follow traditions even though they have independent reasons to believe that those traditions are bad. In experimental settings, there is good evidence that people will follow even arbitrary traditions, failing to bring their own judgments to bear.[7] The basic problem is that traditions convey information, and people may think that the information is more helpful, or more revealing, than it actually is.

In a separate phenomenon, people may know that traditions are bad and have little confidence in the judgments of the past, but nonetheless may adhere to past practices as a result of reputational pressures—ranging from disapproval to ostracism to punishments both formal and informal. Those who deviate from traditions often face serious social sanctions.[8] In any event, there is no reason, in the abstract, to think that long-standing practices are always better than the alternatives proposed by reformers or even extremists.[9]

After all, the American Revolution was not a traditionalist one. Federalist Paper No. 1 offers a direct challenge to Burkeanism with the suggestion: "It has been frequently remarked that it seems to have been reserved to the people of this country, by their conduct and example, to decide the important question, whether societies of men are really capable or not of establishing good government from reflection and choice, or whether they are forever destined to depend for their political constitutions on accident and force." The opposition between "reflection and choice," on the one hand, and "accident and force," on the other, suggests a sharp critique of those who value traditions as repositories of wisdom.

Consider, too, the words of James Madison, writing in a very young America:

> Is it not the glory of the people of America that, whilst they have paid a decent regard to the opinions of former times and other nations, they have not suffered a blind veneration for antiquity,

for custom, or for names, to overrule the suggestions of their own good sense, the knowledge of their own situation, and the lessons of their own experience?[10]

In Madison's unmistakably antitraditionalist account, Americans "accomplished a revolution which has no parallel in the annals of human society. They reared the fabrics of governments which have no model on the face of the globe."[11]

These are largely rhetorical passages, but there is actually an argument in the background, one that turns Burkeanism on its head. Thomas Jefferson himself captured that argument with his objection that some people "ascribe to the men of the preceding age a wisdom more than human." His response, a kind of rebuke, was that the age of the founders "was very like the present, but without the experience of the present; and forty years of experience in government is worth a century of book-reading."[12] Burkeans tend to cherish the wisdom of those long dead, but in Jefferson's view, their stock of wisdom was far more limited than ours. In the same vein, Pascal contended that we are the ancients: "Those whom we call ancient were really new in all things, and properly constituted the infancy of mankind; and as we have joined to their knowledge the experience of the centuries which have followed them, it is in ourselves that we should find this antiquity that we revere in others."[13]

Jeremy Bentham attacked ancient wisdom in identical terms, contending that those who are ancient are, in the relevant sense, very young.[14] Bentham acknowledged that old people have more experience than young people, but he insisted that "as between generation and generation, the reverse of this is true."[15] In fact, "the wisdom of the times called old" is "the wisdom of the cradle."[16] Bentham deplored the "reigning prejudice in favor of the dead" and also the tendency to disparage the present generation, which has a greater stock of knowledge than "untaught, inexperienced generations." Consider in this regard attacks on established practices in such areas as discrimination on the basis of race, sex, and disability. As we have seen, the movements that led to these attacks benefited greatly from group polarization. In many domains, traditionalism is an important constraint on unjustified movements, but too often, traditions are themselves a product of the same sorts of forces that lead people in bad directions.

CONSEQUENCES

A separate approach to the risks associated with group polarization is to call for careful investigation of the consequences of one or another course of action. It is important to see that this approach, associated with Bentham, may or may not check extremism. In the end, the investigation of consequences might support rather than undermine the argument for dramatic steps. But there is nonetheless an important constraint here—a kind of reality check. Consequentialism promises to discipline extreme movements—or, for that matter, enthusiasm for the status quo—by subjecting them to certain tests. The consequentialist hope is that the necessary investigation can dampen social controversy and the risks associated with group polarization by asking people to engage with the facts.[17]

Suppose, for example, that people in a certain neighborhood are becoming frightened about a particular risk, such as crime, pesticides, or electromagnetic fields. If they are stoking one another's fears, it might be useful to ask: Are people really at serious risk? What, exactly, do we know about the size of the risk, and what do we know about the burdens of trying to reduce it? Questions of this kind can prevent a situation in which echo chambers serve to produce unjustified fear of risks that really do not deserve concern.

In the context of government action, an important example involves debates over the role of deterrence in criminal law. Many people think that we should be asking serious questions about the deterrent effect of certain punishments—the death penalty, restrictions on gun ownership, life imprisonment for those who have committed three felonies. Their hope is that if we ask about such issues, we will be able to reduce the intensity of certain conflicts by engaging closely with the facts.[18] If we can agree that the argument for gun control must stand or fall on whether it is effective in reducing crime, then perhaps we can quiet some of our disagreements on that issue. If the death penalty does not deter crime, perhaps we can agree to abolish the death penalty. At the very least, that is the hope of those who seek to put a spotlight on the question of deterrence.

In the regulatory context, where the democratic process is often badly polarized, we can find many examples. Consider, for example, the regulation of arsenic in drinking water. Some people are not concerned by very small levels of arsenic exposure—say, 50 parts per billion. They believe that such small levels cannot possibly deserve social concern or serious sums of money. They think that the government should pay attention to more serious problems. Other people think that arsenic is a poison that is toxic even at low doses, and they believe that the permissible level should be very low—say, 3 parts per billion. We can easily imagine a situation in which the disagreement becomes very intense, as like-minded people talk mostly to one another, stirring themselves up into real antagonism. And in fact, a battle of just this kind occurred over arsenic regulation in 2000.[19]

To those who care about consequences, the best way to proceed is to assess the actual effects of low levels of arsenic exposure and to see how much it would cost to reduce those effects. What is the risk of cancer at 50 parts per billion? Is it one in a million? One in 10,000? If the permissible level is reduced to 3 parts per million, how many lives will be saved per year? And how much will that reduction cost? Will people's water bills increase significantly or, instead, trivially? Answers to these questions might also enable us to find some common ground. In the process, such answers seem to offer a kind of check on various dangers, including interest-group power, confusion, and group polarization. If some groups are calling for no regulation, and others for aggressive regulation, an analysis of consequences might provide helpful, at least if it can restrict the range of reasonable disagreement.[20] If Boulder types insist that certain substances should be banned, and if Colorado Springs types insist that no regulation is the right approach, an investigation of actual effects might serve as an arbiter, or as a demonstration that neither side has it quite right. Consider in this light the highly polarized debate over climate change. Perhaps a careful investigation of the consequences—both of greenhouse gas emissions and of efforts to reduce them—can help a great deal.

In some domains, of course, disputes over consequences can reflect rather than dampen group polarization. Some groups might find, and argue, that the benefits of certain steps are low and that the costs are high; other groups might press the opposite conclusions. In the history of federal regulation, it is hardly unusual to see different sides invoking their view of consequences in favor of radically different conclusions. Consisting solely or mostly of like-minded types, some groups might conclude that the analysis clearly justifies some kind of regulation, whereas other groups might conclude that the same analysis justifies nothing at all. Disputes over climate change certainly reflect conflicts of exactly this sort.[21] Group polarization is undoubtedly a contributor to those conflicts. But even in the domain of climate change, where so many questions remain open, an analysis of the consequences can impose a valuable discipline. It suggests, for example, that global inaction is quite indefensible, and also that there are limits to how aggressively we should cut emissions in the near future.[22]

Bitter debates over occupational safety, disability rights, national security, and affirmative action—to say the least, polarizing issues—might well be rendered somewhat less hot with a better understanding of the consequences of one approach or another. Of course, it is especially likely, in those domains, that polarization will be replicated, not diminished, as different groups attempt to assess consequences. But the great promise of the inquiry is that the range of reasonable disagreement can be narrowed—and that when people take strong stands, it will be after engagement with actual effects, rather than solely a product of social interactions.

CHECKS AND BALANCES

A third answer, and perhaps the most valuable, emerges from an investigation of the American founding. To understand that answer, it is important to see that the founding period witnessed an extraordinary debate over the nature of republican institutions. What kinds of institutions would best suit the young nation? That question was debated in part by reference to the views of the political theorist Montesquieu, who was a revered source for all sides and a central figure in the development of the idea of separation of powers.

The antifederalists, eloquent opponents of the proposed constitution, complained that the document's framers had betrayed Montesquieu by attempting to create a powerful central government, one that could not possibly manage a diverse nation. Brutus, an especially articulate antifederalist, spoke for the republican tradition when he urged: "In a republic, the manners, sentiments, and interests of the people should be similar. If this be not the case, there will be constant clashing of opinions; and the representatives of one part will be continually striving against those of the other."[23]

Those who favored the constitution believed that Brutus had it exactly backward. Skeptical about uniformity of opinion, they affirmatively welcomed diversity, disagreement, and the "constant clashing of opinions." They sought a situation in which "the representatives of one part will be continually striving against those of the other." Alexander Hamilton spoke most clearly on the point, urging that the "differences of opinion, and the jarring of parties in [the legislative] department of the government ... often promote deliberation and circumspection; and serve to check the excesses of the majority."[24] As the framers stressed, widespread error is likely to result when like-minded people, insulated from others, deliberate on their own. In their view, heterogeneity of view can be a protective force. A constitution that ensures the "jarring of parties" and "differences of opinion" can provide safeguards against unjustified movements of view.

More particularly, the institutions of our Constitution reflect an implicit fear of polarization, creating a range of checks on potentially ill-considered judgments. The most obvious example is bicameralism. The idea of a bicameral legislature was designed as a safeguard against a situation in which one house—in the framers' view, most likely the House of Representatives—would be overcome by short-term passions and even group polarization. In the founding period, the Senate was thought to be especially important in this regard. Consider the widely reported story that on his return from France, Thomas Jefferson called George Washington to account at the breakfast table for having agreed to a second chamber. "Why," asked Washington, "did you pour that coffee into your saucer?" "To cool it," quoth Jefferson. "Even so," said Washington, "we pour legislation into the senatorial saucer to cool it."[25] James Wilson's great lectures on law spoke of bicameralism very much in these terms, referring to "instances, in which the people have become the miserable victims of passions, operating on their government without restraint" and seeing a "single legislature" as prone to "sudden and violent fits of despotism, injustice, and cruelty."[26]

We can understand many aspects of the system of checks and balances in the same general terms. The duty to present legislation to the president protects against polarization effects within the legislative branch.[27] The opportunity for presidential veto supplements the system of bicameralism, further reducing the risk of hasty or ill-considered legislation. The very fact that the president cannot make law on his own, and must rely on Congress for authorization, creates a crucial safeguard against the potentially disastrous effects of group polarization within the executive branch. Compare dictatorships and tyrannies, which concentrate political power within a single branch, prone to grotesque error, in part because of polarization. And because law cannot operate against citizens without the concurrence of the legislative and executive branches, enacting and then enforcing the law, there is a further safeguard.

Federalism itself was, and remains, an engine of diversity, creating "circuit breakers" in the form of a variety of sovereigns with separate cultures. In the federal system, social influences may produce error in some states, and states can certainly fall into cascades. But the existence of separate systems creates a check on the diffusion of error. In this respect, federalism permits states to restrain one another. A particularly important part of this process involves the right to exit. If one state oppresses its citizens, there is always the freedom to leave. That very freedom creates a before-the-fact deterrent to oppressive legislation. It also creates an after-the-fact safeguard. In this sense, the right to travel, from one sovereign to another, is first and foremost a political right, akin to the right to vote itself. And if a form of group polarization occurs in one state, the federal system ensures that other states will come to different views. Here, too, we can find a safeguard of liberty.

An understanding of group polarization also casts fresh light on one of the most important and controversial provisions in the American Constitution: the grant of power to Congress, and not the president, to "declare war."[28] The debates in the framing period suggest a fear of two risks: The president might make war without sufficient authorization from the citizenry, and he might do so without sufficient deliberation and debate among diverse people. Thus Pinckney urged that the Senate "would be the best depository, being more acquainted with foreign affairs, and most capable of proper resolutions."[29] Butler, by contrast, sought to vest the power of war in the president, urging that he "will have all the requisite qualities, and will not make war but when the Nation will support it."[30] Madison and Gerry made the key compromise, suggesting that Congress should have the power to "declare" war. This provision was understood to permit the president "to repel sudden attacks."[31] But otherwise, the president would be required to seek congressional approval, in part on the theory that (in Mason's words) this would amount "to clogging rather than facilitating war" and to "facilitating peace."[32]

If warmaking is seen to be an especially grave act, we might be especially troubled about permitting the president to make war on his own. This is not at all because the president is immune from political checks. It is because group dynamics within the executive branch create a risk of polarization, as like-minded people push one another to indefensible extremes. We have seen that the executive branch is distinctly at risk here, at least to the extent that presidents create Teams of Unrivals who reinforce, and do not contest, the initial inclinations of their leaders. A requirement of congressional authorization ensures a check from another institution, with diverse voices and a degree of independence from the executive branch.

Of course, the system of free expression is fundamental to the process. Unjustified extremism, in government and outside it, can be met by opposing voices. The First Amendment has a checking function;[33] it is part and parcel of checks and balances. Those who are tempted to adopt extreme positions, perhaps as a result of group polarization, can be countered by others who believe that their facts and their values are wrong, or at least are missing something important. So long as people are listening to one another, free speech should ensure that when extreme movements occur, it is not because dissenting voices have not been heard.

These points have significant lessons for how to combat risks of violence, including terrorism. If terrorism results from a process of radicalization in which like-minded people congregate, a response is to interject moderate or dissenting voices, preferably from trusted sources. In "Muslim enclaves," the "battle is completely one-sided. The true believers, who populate the radical forums, are working themselves into a frenzy with no moderate voice present to calm them down. This leads to ever greater radicalization on the part of the participants, who slowly take on the views of their friends."[34] The countless "Muslims who reject violence need to enter this arena and participate in the discussions to influence and stop this slide toward ever greater radicalization."[35]

DELIBERATIVE DEMOCRACY AND THE WISDOM OF CROWDS

In the last decades, a great deal of attention has been given to the idea of "deliberative democracy."[36] The central idea is that well-functioning democracies do not rely on snapshots of public opinion or on what most people think should be done. Instead, they attempt to combine deliberation and reason-giving with accountability. They insist that public action should follow a process in which people exchange information and ideas.

An understanding of group polarization raises some serious cautionary notes about deliberative democracy. It is foolish to celebrate deliberation as such or to believe that groups will arrive at truth or even sense. The exchange of information and ideas can and does breed unjustified extremism. Groups often blunder precisely because they put a high premium on deliberation.

Consider in this light the recent enthusiasm for the wisdom of crowds.[37] The key claim here is that if you take the median or average view of a group of people, that view will often be stunningly accurate—far more accurate than the view of the overwhelming majority of group members. The accuracy of judgments of statistical groups can often be explained by reference to the Condorcet Jury Theorem, which offers one of the most interesting results in modern social theory.[38] To see how the Jury Theorem works, suppose that people are answering the same question with two possible answers, one false and one true. Assume, too, that the probability that each voter will answer correctly exceeds 50 percent. The Jury Theorem says that the probability of a correct answer, by a majority of the group, increases toward 100 percent as the size of the group increases. The key point is that groups will do better than individuals, and big groups better than little ones, so long as two conditions are met: Majority rule is used, and each person is more likely than not to be correct.

The Jury Theorem is based on some fairly simple arithmetic. Suppose, for example, that there is a three-person group in which each member has a 67 percent probability of being right. The probability that a majority vote will produce the correct answer is 74 percent.[39] As the size of the group increases, this probability increases, too. It should be clear that as the likelihood of a correct answer by individual members increases, the likelihood of a correct answer by the group increases, too, at least if majority rule is used. If group members are 80 percent likely to be right, and if the group contains ten or more people, the probability of a correct answer by the majority is overwhelmingly high—very close to 100 percent.

The Jury Theorem suggests that large groups can often be wise indeed. But there is a dark side to the Jury Theorem, and it, too, has important implications. Suppose that each individual in a group is more likely to be wrong than right. If so, the likelihood that the group's majority will decide correctly falls to *zero* as the size of the group increases!

Imagine that an organization consists of a number of people, each of whom is at least 51 percent likely to be mistaken. The organization might be a political party, a religious group, a university faculty, or a terrorist group. The probability that the organization will err approaches 100 percent as the size of the group expands. Condorcet explicitly signaled this possibility and its source: "In effect, when the probability of the truth of a voter's opinion falls below 1/2, there must be a reason why he decides less well than one would at random. The reason can only be found in the prejudices to which this voter is subject."[40] The errors might stem not only from "prejudices" but also from confusion and incompetence. On tricky math problems, there is no reason to think that the average answer of a large group will be right. So, too, on complex issues involving politics. And even if people are competent, they might well be led astray, especially if they are subject to "prejudices" or if they are dealing with highly technical questions.

Now let us return to the topic of deliberation. Even if the average view of a large group is likely to be right, a process of deliberation might skew people's judgments, leading to major errors. As people influence one another, a bias might creep into the group's thinking, leading it astray. We have encountered many examples. In some circumstances, deliberation actually produces a serious distortion. Groups often do pretty well if they take the average answer, without deliberation; under bad conditions, the average answer will get worse after they have spoken to one another.

But I do not mean to challenge deliberative conceptions of democracy here or to suggest that businesses, families, religious organizations, and unions would do better simply to take polls. An understanding of group polarization does not justify that radical conclusion. It suggests only that we need to specify the idea of deliberation, rather than to celebrate it as such. A system of deliberation is likely to work well if it includes diverse people—that is, if it has a degree of diversity in terms of approaches, information, and positions.[41] Cognitive diversity is crucial to the success of deliberative democracy and its analogues in the private sector.

A NOTE ON GROUP POLARIZATION AND WAR

Luther Gulick was a high-level official in the Roosevelt administration during World War II. In 1948, a few years after the Allied victory, Gulick delivered a series of lectures, unimaginatively titled *Administrative Reflections from World War II*, which offered, in some (tedious) detail, a set of observations about bureaucratic structure and administrative reform.[42] In a brief and far from tedious epilogue, Gulick set out to compare the warmaking capacities of democracies with those of their Fascist adversaries.

Gulick began by noting that the initial evaluation of the United States, among the leaders of Germany and Japan, was "not flattering."[43] We were, in their view, "incapable of quick or effective national action even in our own defense because under democracy we were divided by our polyglot society and under capitalism deadlocked by our conflicting private interests."[44] Our adversaries said that we could not fight. They believed what they said. And dictatorships did seem to have real advantages. They were free of delays, inertia, and sharp internal divisions. They did not have to reckon, on a continuing basis, with the opinions of a mass of citizens, some with little education and little intelligence. Dictatorships could also rely on a single leader and an integrated hierarchy, making it easier to develop national unity and enthusiasm, to overcome surprise, and to act vigorously and with dispatch. But these claims about the advantages of totalitarian regimes turned out to be bogus.

The United States and its allies performed far better than Germany, Italy, and Japan. Gulick linked their superiority directly to democracy itself. In particular, he emphasized "the kind of review and criticism which democracy alone affords."[45] With a totalitarian regime, plans "are hatched in secret by a small group of partially informed men and then enforced through dictatorial authority."[46] Such plans are likely to contain fatal weaknesses. By contrast, a democracy allows wide criticism and debate, thus avoiding "many a disaster." In a totalitarian system, criticisms and suggestions are neither wanted nor heeded. "Even the leaders tend to believe their own propaganda. All of the stream of authority and information is from the top down," so that when change is needed, the high command never learns of that need. But in a democracy, "the public and the press have no hesitation in observing and criticizing the first evidence of failure once a program has been put into operation."[47] In a democracy, information flows within the government—between the lowest and highest ranks—and via public opinion.

With a combination of melancholy and surprise, Gulick noted that the United States and its allies did not show more unity than Germany, Japan, and Italy. "The gregarious social impulses of men around the world are apparently much the same, giving rise to the same reactions of group loyalty when men are subjected to the same true or imagined group threats."[48] Top-down management of mass morale, by the German and Japanese leaders, actually worked. Dictatorships are not less successful in war because of less loyalty or more distrust from the public. They are less successful because their leaders do not receive the checks and corrections that come from democratic processes.

Gulick is offering a claim here about how institutions perform better when challenges are frequent, when people do not stifle themselves, and when information flows freely. Of course, Gulick is providing his personal account of a particular set of events, and he does not really demonstrate that success in war is a product of democratic institutions. The Soviet Union, for example, fought valiantly and well, even under the tyranny of Stalin. But Gulick's general theme contains a great deal of truth. Careful studies show that democracies do especially well in fighting wars.[49] One reason is that democracies do not start wars if they are not likely to win. A more interesting reason, fitting with Gulick's theme, is that because of individual liberty, democracies will have better access to accurate information, so that they are able to correct mistaken courses of action.

There is a more general point here. Institutions are far more likely to succeed if they subject leaders to critical scrutiny and if they ensure that courses of action will face continuing monitoring and review from outsiders—if, in short, they use diversity and dissent to reduce the risks of error that come from group polarization.

DIVERSITY AND BALANCE

The idea of checks and balances is an old one, but it can be used innovatively. In the United States, a great deal of national policy is established by the so-called independent regulatory commissions, such as the Federal Communications Commission (FCC), the Federal Trade Commission, the Securities and Exchange Commission, and the National Labor Relations Board. These agencies typically consist of five members, who are appointed by the president (with the advice and consent of the Senate), serve for specified terms (usually seven years), and make decisions by majority vote. Because of the immense importance of their decisions, any Democratic president would much like to be able to ensure that the commissions consist entirely or almost entirely of Democratic appointees; Republican presidents would certainly like to shift policy in their preferred directions by ensuring domination by Republican appointees.

Under existing law, however, presidential control of the commissions is sharply constrained, for no more than a bare majority can be from a single political party. Congress has explicitly so required, and indeed, this has become the standard pattern for the independent agencies. Hence, for example, the National Labor Relations Board (NLRB) and the Federal Communications Commission must consist either of three Republicans and two Democrats or of three Democrats and two Republicans. From the standpoint of the president, a particular problem arises in a time of transition from one administration to the next. A Democratic president, for example, is often disturbed to learn that agencies entrusted with implementing legislation policy will have at least two Republicans (appointed by his predecessor).

It should be clear that the requirement of bipartisan composition operates as a constraint on group polarization and extreme movements. Five Democratic appointees to the NLRB, for example, might well lead national labor law in dramatic new directions. To this extent, bipartisan member-ship serves to limit unwarrantedly extreme changes in regu-latory policy. We can understand the requirement as an effort to ensure against group polarization—as an effort to reduce the risk that when labor law is moving in significant ways, it is simply because of social interactions among like-minded people.

Do similar considerations apply to the federal judiciary? At first glance, the judiciary is quite different, because many people believe that it is not supposed to make policy at all. But the evidence reveals a more complicated picture. We have seen that extreme movements are shown by DDD and RRR panels, in the sense that judges, on such panels, are especially likely to vote in line with ideological stereotypes.

A controversial implication is that in the most difficult and ideologically charged cases, those who seek to avoid the effects of group polarization should consider diverse judicial panels, as in the context of the NLRB and the FCC. This implication is controversial because the judiciary is not understood as a policy-making institution, because such an approach might cement judicial self-identification in political terms, and because efforts to ensure ideological diversity might well be taken as inconsistent with the commitment to judicial neutrality. But the discussion here suggests that judges are policy makers of a distinctive kind and that in principle, the argument for diversity, as a means of counteracting group polarization, is not significantly different from the argument in the context of the independent regulatory commissions. Recall that while the NLRB must be DDDRR or RRRDD, reviewing courts are not similarly constrained, and that the ultimate fate of NLRB decisions and hence national labor law, even in the most important domains, will often be radically different if the reviewing court is RRR or DDD. By contrast, appellate panels are far more moderate if they are RRD or RDD.

This example has general implications. In many domains, private and public institutions consist of like-minded people; they are akin to our experimental groups in Boulder, to RRR panels, to the White House under George W. Bush, even to social networks consisting entirely of angry Muslims. Well-functioning groups attempt to ensure a diversity of views, if only to protect themselves against blunders and confusion. If teams of doctors want to make accurate diagnoses, they will promote a norm of skepticism, even among younger and less experienced members.[50] If corporations want to avoid disaster, they do best to create diverse boards that do not defer to the CEO. A close observer of corporate failures concludes that one remedy lies in "strong, high-functioning work groups whose members . . . challenge one another and engage directly with senior managers on critical issues facing corporations."[51] The problem is that when corporate directors, even intelligent and powerful ones, are placed "into a group that discourages dissent, they nearly always start to conform." And "CEOs who don't welcome dissent try to pack the court." This is a serious problem for shareholders because the evidence suggests that "the highest performing companies have extremely contentious boards that regard dissent as an obligation and that treat no subject as undiscussable." Thus well-functioning boards contain "clashing viewpoints and challenging questions."

These points are a tribute to the power of checks and balances—to the value of creating Teams of Rivals, even in domains in which leaders usually seek team players, that is, those who go along with prevailing wisdom. If unjustified extremism is a problem, the old idea of checks and balances is likely to have a number of fresh uses. We have only started to realize its promise.

CHAPTER 5

Good Extremism

It is obvious that extremism is not always bad. Sometimes extreme movements are good, even great. When people shift from indifference to intense concern with local problems, such as poverty and crime, group polarization is an achievement, not a problem. Barry Goldwater was correct to say that "extremism in the defense of liberty is no vice." The American Revolution, the civil rights movement, and the fall of both communism and apartheid had everything to do with mechanisms of the sort sketched here. Once we acknowledge that extremism can be desirable, and that group polarization can move people toward engagement in solving serious problems, the analysis has to be modified. But how?

DIVERSITIES

Societies gain from group polarization and, in particular, from deliberating enclaves, consisting of groups of like-minded people. People need spaces where they can assemble with others to discuss issues on their own; consider, for example, entrepreneurs, scientists, disabled people, economists, and the elderly. Such spaces promote learning, creativity, and innovation. They provide comfort and solace. They are also indispensable to both economic growth and democracy. In an important essay, law professor Heather Gerken draws attention to "second-order diversity"—the kind of diversity that comes when society consists of many groups that do not have a lot of internal diversity.[1] First-order diversity has been my emphasis here; it refers to the degree of diversity *within* groups and organizations. Second-order diversity is altogether different. It refers to the degree of diversity *across* groups and organizations.

The United States gains from a situation in which Utah, California, and Massachusetts are allowed to attempt their own experiments on marriage, welfare, and the environment. We can all see what works and what doesn't. If some economics departments are conservative and others are liberal, the profession as a whole, and eventually the nation, will learn from the ideas and theories that emerge. Gerken argues that in many domains, what we do seek, and what we should seek, is second-order diversity. John Stuart Mill celebrated "experiments in living,"[2] and any such experiments will ensure that like-minded types spend a lot of time together. And when second-order diversity exists, there will be a number of echo chambers—and a lot of group polarization.

For any nation, second-order diversity may be especially important, certainly in the long run. If many organizations are allowed to exist, and if each of them is made up of like-minded people, the nation will ultimately benefit from the greater range of views and practices that emerge. Inevitably, several of those groups will be extreme, but their very extremism will enrich society's "argument pool" and thus promote sensible solutions. The federal system benefits from second-order diversity; so does the study of science, anthropology, and literature. Freedom of association ensures the existence of a wide range of like-minded groups: Catholic organizations, Jewish organizations, animal rights groups, the National Rifle Association, gay rights groups, pro-Palestinian groups, Muslim organizations, and countless more. If group polarization is occurring in some or many of those groups, we may all gain from what emerges.

There is a further point. If people speak to like-minded others, they are more likely to be energized, and if they are more likely to be energized, they are more likely to become active, politically or otherwise.[3] If people hear the other side and give serious consideration to competing arguments, they may well be more respectful and tolerant—but they are also more likely to be passive and perhaps even indifferent. Group polarization promotes engagement; conversations with multiple others can produce inaction and paralysis. A political process might well depend on a situation in which many groups of like-minded types spur their members to seek change.

ENCLAVES AND SELF-SILENCING

Enclaves provide many benefits for their members and for society alike. I received a powerful lesson about those benefits twenty years ago in Beijing, when I taught a class to a group of about forty highly educated men and women on the topic of sex equality and feminism. In a session of about two hours, only the men spoke. Almost all of them were hostile to feminism. No woman said a single word. After the session, I asked some of the women why they had been silent. One of them said, "In China, we are taught that to speak out is not beautiful." In private discussions, it emerged that many of the women in the room had strong feminist commitments, believed that China did not promote sex equality, and agreed with the basic thrust of feminist arguments as they were made in American law schools. These positions emerged in small groups. They were not much voiced in larger ones, at least if significant numbers of men were present. But they are now playing a large role in Chinese society.

This is not only a story about China. Even in the United States, Canada, and Europe, women sometimes silence themselves, notwithstanding the success of the movement for equality. The same is true for members of many other groups, including African Americans and religious conservatives. Such silence does serious harm to group members and the public at large. The silence deprives society of information that it needs to have. In this light, a special advantage of what we might call "enclave deliberation" is that it promotes the development of positions that would otherwise be invisible, silenced, or squelched in general debate.

In numerous contexts, this is a great advantage. Many social movements have been made possible through this route; consider the civil rights movement, Reaganism, the disability rights movement, environmentalism, the movement for gay and lesbian rights, and both gun control and opposition to gun control. The efforts of marginalized groups to exclude outsiders, and even the efforts of political parties to limit their primaries to party members, can be understood and sometimes justified in similar terms. Even if group polarization is at work—perhaps *because* group polarization is at work—enclaves can provide a wide range of social benefits, especially to the extent that they enrich the number of available facts and arguments. And when members of such groups eventually speak in more heterogeneous groups, they often do so with greater clarity and confidence. Society ends up knowing a lot more than it knew before.

A central empirical point is that in deliberating bodies, high-status members tend to initiate communication more than others, and their ideas are more influential, partly because low-status members lack confidence in their own abilities, and partly because they fear retribution.[4] For example, women's ideas are often less influential and sometimes "suppressed altogether in mixed-gender groups."[5] In ordinary circumstances, cultural minorities have disproportionately little influence on decisions by culturally mixed groups.[6] In these circumstances, it makes sense to promote deliberating enclaves in which members of multiple groups may speak with one another and develop their views.

But there is a serious danger in such enclaves. The danger is that through group polarization, members will move to positions that lack merit but are predictable consequences of the particular circumstances of enclave deliberation. We have seen that in extreme cases, enclave deliberation may end up in violence and put social stability at risk. And it is impossible to say, in the abstract, that those who sort themselves into enclaves will generally move in a direction that is desirable for society at large or even for themselves. It is easy to think of examples to the contrary; consider the rise of Nazism, hate groups, conspiracy theorists, terrorist cells, and numerous cults of various sorts.

Sometimes the threat to social stability is desirable. As Thomas Jefferson wrote, turbulence can be "productive of good. It prevents the degeneracy of government, and nourishes a general attention to ... public affairs. I hold ... that a little rebellion now and then is a good thing."[7] Turbulence to one side, any judgments about enclave deliberation are hard to make without a sense of the underlying substance—of what it is that divides the enclave from the rest of society. Note once more that nothing is wrong with group polarization by itself: If people become more outraged after talking, if punitive damage awards go up, or if people end up with a stronger commitment to the position with which they began, nothing need be amiss. We cannot condemn movements toward new points of view without knowing whether the new points of view are better or worse.

From the standpoint of designing our institutions and even living our daily lives, one problem is that enclave deliberation will ensure group polarization among a wide range of groups—some necessary to the pursuit of justice, others likely to promote injustice, and still others potentially quite dangerous. And even when enclaves lead in good directions, enclave deliberation is unlikely to produce change unless its members are eventually brought into contact with others. In democratic societies, the best approach, and the way to benefit from second-order diversity, is to ensure that any such enclaves are not walled off from competing views—and that at many points, there is an exchange of views between enclave members and those who disagree with them.

It is total or near-total self-insulation, rather than group deliberation as such, that carries with it the most serious dangers—often in the highly unfortunate (and sometimes literally deadly) combination of extremism with marginality. One of the most important lessons is among the most general: It is crucial to create spaces for enclave deliberation without insulating enclave members from those with opposing views and without insulating those outside the enclave from the views of those within it. But how might we go beyond these abstractions?

FREE SPEECH, PUBLIC FORUMS, AND THE ARCHITECTURE OF SERENDIPITY

In a common understanding, the free speech principle forbids government from "censoring" speech of which it disapproves. In the standard cases, the government attempts to impose penalties, whether civil or criminal, on political dissent, libelous speech, commercial advertising, or sexually explicit speech. The question is whether the government is allowed to restrict the speech that it seeks to control; in free societies, usually it isn't.

This is indeed what most of the law of free speech is about. But in many free nations, an important part of free speech law takes a quite different form; it has a positive dimension. In the United States, for example, the Supreme Court has ruled that streets and parks must be kept open to the public for expressive activity. In the leading case, from the first half of the twentieth century, the Court said, "Wherever the title of streets and parks may rest, they have immemorially been held in trust for the use of the public and time out of mind, have been used for the purposes of assembly, communicating thought between citizens, and discussing public questions. Such use of the streets and public places has, from ancient times, been a part of the privileges, immunities, rights, and liberties of citizens."[8] Hence governments are obliged to allow speech to occur freely on public streets and in public parks—even if many citizens would prefer to have peace and quiet, and even if it seems irritating to come across protestors and dissidents when you are simply walking home or to the local grocery store.

To understand the relationship between the public forum doctrine and unjustified extremism, we should notice that the public forum doctrine promotes some important social goals.[9] First, it ensures that speakers can have access to a wide array of people who might otherwise live in their own enclaves. If you want to claim that taxes are too high or that police brutality against African Americans is widespread, you are able to press this argument on many people who would otherwise not hear the message. The diverse people who walk the streets and use the parks are likely to hear speakers' arguments about taxes or the police; they might also learn about the nature and intensity of views held by their fellow citizens. Perhaps some people's views change because of what they learn; perhaps they will become curious enough to investigate the question on their own. On the speakers' side, the public forum doctrine thus creates a right of general access to heterogeneous citizens.

On the listeners' side, the public forum creates not exactly a right but an opportunity, if perhaps an unwelcome one: shared exposure to diverse speakers with diverse views and complaints. It is important to emphasize that the exposure is shared. Many people will be simultaneously exposed to the same views and complaints, and they will encounter views and complaints that some of them might have refused to seek out in the first instance. Indeed, the exposure might well be considered, much of the time, irritating or worse.

Second, the public forum doctrine allows speakers to have general access not only to heterogeneous people but also to specific people and specific institutions with whom they have a complaint and who might otherwise be insulated from that complaint. Suppose, for example, that you believe that the state legislature has behaved irresponsibly with respect to health care for children. The public forum ensures that you can make your views heard by legislators, simply by protesting in front of the state legislature itself.

The point applies to private as well as public institutions. If a clothing store is believed to have cheated customers or to have acted in a racist manner, protestors are allowed a form of access to the store itself. This is not because they have a right to trespass on private property—no one has such a right—but because a public street is highly likely to be close by, and a strategically located protest will undoubtedly catch the attention of the store and its customers. Under the public forum doctrine, speakers are thus permitted to have access to particular audiences, and particular listeners cannot easily avoid hearing complaints that are directed against them. In other words, listeners have a sharply limited power of self-insulation.

Third, and most important, the public forum doctrine increases the likelihood that people generally will be exposed to a wide variety of people and views. When you go to work or visit a park, it is possible that you will have a range of unexpected encounters, however fleeting or seemingly inconsequential. On your way to the office or when eating lunch in the park, you cannot easily wall yourself off from contentions or conditions that you would not have sought out in advance or that you would avoided if you could. Here, too, the public forum doctrine tends to ensure a range of experiences that are widely shared—streets and parks are public property—and also a set of exposures to diverse views and conditions.

The public forum doctrine reflects a kind of social architecture, meant in the literal sense. It works to counteract a situation in which members of deliberating groups are engaged in a high degree of self-segregation. I have referred to the architecture of serendipity and opposed it to the architecture of control. The public forum doctrine opposes control and promotes serendipity. It ensures a range of unplanned, unanticipated, unchosen encounters. In that way, it promotes cognitive diversity. It makes it difficult for like-minded people to insulate themselves from those who think differently. Indeed, the architecture of serendipity is part of a well-functioning system of checks and balances; it helps to check the effects of echo chambers and ensure that those with blinders, or those who prefer information cocoons, occasionally see elsewhere. What they see may change their minds, even their lives.

CHECKS AND BALANCES EVERYWHERE

Is it possible to generalize from the public forum doctrine? We might be able to think of other domains in which people might benefit from serendipity and in which social architecture can ensure that people who spend a lot of time in enclaves are also exposed to competing views. Daily newspapers, weekly newsmagazines, and radio and television broadcasters can do a great deal of good on this count. When they are operating well, they combat unjustified extremism by ensuring that like-minded people will occasionally see things that seem jarring and that might make them rethink. To the extent that private institutions are aware of the risks that I have discussed, they assume a civic or democratic function precisely in the sense that they see themselves as a key part of the system of checks and balances. In the 1980s, Mark Fowler, the head of the Federal Communications Commission, said, "Television is just another appliance. . . . It's a toaster with pictures." If the mass media sees itself in these terms, it may well promote, rather than reduce, the difficulties I have explored here.[10] A central task, in democratic societies, is for the print and broadcast media, and those who run and participate in Web sites, to combat self-segregation along political or other lines.

It would also be most valuable to take a fresh look at other institutions that either promote or combat self-insulation. I have referred to the fact that bipartisan membership is required for some of the most important institutions in the United States: the National Labor Relations Board, the Federal Communications Commission, the Federal Trade Commission, the Securities and Exchange Commission. If the goal is to undermine (false) conspiracy theories, a good means is to ensure that those who hold such theories are exposed to credible counterarguments and are not living in an echo chamber of their own design.[11] In the private sector, economic disasters, for individuals and large groups, are often a product of conversations among like-minded people, in which some investment or project seems to be a sure winner. The economic crisis that began in 2008 was a product, in significant part, of a form of group polarization, in which skeptics about the real estate bubble, armed with statistical evidence, did not receive a fair hearing or were in a sense silenced. The best companies, and the best investors, benefit from internal checks and balances.[12]

I have emphasized that extreme movements may be desirable, even when they result from mechanisms of the sort traced here. And even when they are not desirable, extreme positions can do a great deal of good. Societies gain from second-order diversity, not least because of the range of experiments, and the vast array of competing positions, produced by that form of diversity. Nothing said here is meant to deny these claims. But if extreme movements are to occur, it should be because they are sensible and right— and not because of the predictable effects of interactions among the like-minded.

Appendix: Findings of Group Polarization

It is an understatement to say that the literature on group polarization is vast. To give a sense of the variety and range of the empirical findings, here is a list of some of the most striking experiments.

1. *Polarization of young French men.* After young men in France discussed their opinions of de Gaulle and of Americans, they became polarized in both directions. Initially mildly favorable opinions of de Gaulle turned more favorable, and a slight initial view that "American economic aid is always used for political purposes" became more negative.
   —Serge Moscovici and Marisa Zavalloni, The Group as a Polarizer of Attitudes, *J. Personality & Soc. Psychol.* 12 (1969): 125, 125–35.

2. *Feminists and "chauvinists."* After initially questioning about their opinions on the role of women, a gender-mixed group was divided into liberal and conservative camps. After discussion, the moderately profeminist group became more profeminist. (The initially "chauvinist" group became more chauvinistic, but not to a statistically significant degree.)
   —David G. Myers, Discussion-Induced Attitude Polarization, *Hum. Rel.* 28 (1975): 699, 707–11.

3. *Racial prejudice.* After being questioned about racial prejudice, people were divided into two groups. Then, the "more prejudiced" and "less prejudiced" groups discussed questions such as whether white racism was responsible for the conditions faced by African Americans in American

cities. After discussion, both groups became more polarized toward their respective poles, amplifying disagreement.
—David G. Myers and George D. Bishop, Discussion Effects on Racial Attitudes, *Science* 169 (1970): 778, 778–79.

4. *Risk-taking among business students.* Male business students were asked about the minimum probability of success they would require in order to advise a client to make a risky financial decision. They gave an individual answer and then discussed the decision in groups. The group consensus was to accept significantly more risk than the individual judgments had advised.
—James A. F. Stoner, A Comparison of Individual and Group Decisions Including Risk (July 31, 1961) (unpublished M.S. thesis, Massachusetts Institute of Technology) (on file with the Massachusetts Institute of Technology Library), available at http://hdl.handle.net/1721.1/11330.

5. *Cautious shifts in marriage decisions.* Some group discussions result in cautious, rather than risky, shifts. A cautious shift was observed when people were asked whether, in light of knowing that a female friend had not been getting along well with her fiancé, it was wise for her to marry. The group consensus was less likely to recommend marriage than the individual judgments.
—Ibid., 4.

6. *Cautious shifts and the sick friend.* A cautious shift was also identified when people were asked whether a friend of theirs, about to embark on a long trip but suddenly ill, should actually take the trip. Postdeliberation judgments were less likely to recommend the travel.
—James A. F. Stoner, Risky and Cautious Shifts in Group Decisions, *J. Experimental Soc. Psychol.* 4 (1968): 442, 442–59.

7. *Cautious shifts, and risky ones, among burglars.* When evaluating a site's vulnerability individually, burglars find it more vulnerable (easier to burglarize) than when vulnerability is evaluated in groups. Apparently group members point out "risk cues" to each other, and thus become more apprehensive. At the same time, burglars in groups appear likely to take riskier actions than acting alone.
—Paul F. Cromwell et al., Group Effects on Decision-Making by Burglars, *Psychol. Rep.* 69 (1991): 579, 579–88.

8. *Punitive damage awards.* The punitive damage verdicts of mock juries, after group deliberation, are higher than the median view of individual jurors.

—David Schkade et al., Deliberating about Dollars: The Severity Shift, *Colum. L. Rev.* 100 (2000): 1139, 1139–76.

9. *Jury views of defendant's innocence.* Juries' decisions of guilt and innocence become polarized. People were presented with descriptions of felony cases, written to give a strong or low indication of guilt. Subjects were asked, as individuals, to rate the degree of guilt on a scale from 0 to 20, and then subjects deliberated on mock panels. In the "high guilt" cases, the jury's rating of degree of guilt increased (meaning the defendant was more likely to be guilty), and in the "low guilt" cases, the rating decreased.
—David G. Myers and Martin F. Kaplan, Group-Induced Polarization in Simulated Juries, *Personality & Soc. Psychol. Bull.* 2 (1976): 63, 63–66.

10. *Purchasing decisions of housewives.* Housewives were asked whether they would be a product in cases in which it was not clear that the product would work as promised. They were more willing to make risky purchase decisions after group discussion.
—Arch G. Woodside, Informal Group Influence on Risk Taking, *J. Marketing Res.* 9 (1972): 223, 223–25.

11. *Risky and cautious shifts among blackjack players.* Individual risk takers (blackjack players) shift toward increased risk-taking if the other players in their group make riskier bets (the risky shift)—and shift toward decreased risk-taking if the other players make lower bets (the cautious shift).
—Jim Blascovich et al., Blackjack, Choice Shifts in the Field, *Sociometry* 39 (1976): 274, 274–76.

12. *Altruism in the dictator game.* In the team dictator game, two members of a group of four dictate the division of money among the four. This game is distinguished from the individual dictator game, in which one member of a pair dictates the division. The teams turn out to be more altruistic than individuals. In other words, the more altruistic member of the team (who individually would give more money away) dominates the decision-making process. One hypothesis is that individuals are more likely to act in a socially desirable (altruistic) way as the number of observers increases.
—Timothy N. Cason and Vai-Lam Mui, A Laboratory Study in Group Polarisation in the Team Dictator Game, *Econ. J.* 107 (1997): 1465, 1465–83.

13. *More risky shifts, with violent effects.* Experimenters offered a hypothetical account of police brutality against African Americans and then asked a group of subjects what action to take, with seven choices ranging from

no action to a demonstration in which there is a likelihood of injury to participants. After discussion, the group was more likely to take the riskier and potentially more violent action.
—Norris R. Johnson et al., Crowd Behavior as "Risky Shift": A Laboratory Experiment, *Sociometry* 40 (1977): 183, 183–87.

14. *Church members' growing extremism.* About a hundred church members were given a survey of sixteen church-related opinion statements, such as "ministers should feel free to take a stand from the pulpit on a political issue." Three weeks later, 169 other church members were given either the average of the hundred responses or a frequency distribution of the hundred responses, and then asked to make their own responses. They showed significantly more extreme attitudes than the original hundred.
—David G. Myers et al., Attitude Comparison: Is There Ever a Bandwagon Effect? *J. Applied Soc. Psychol.* 7 (1977): 341, 341–47.

15. *Correlation between choice shifts and the number of risky arguments.* When a greater number of "risky" arguments are presented, the group consensus is more likely to be risk-inclined. In one experiment, groups were asked to discuss arguments for a choice. In those groups that discussed a greater number of risky arguments, the group consensus was more likely to show a risky shift over individual positions. In a similar experiment, subjects were asked to listen to a set of arguments about the questions they had faced (which, they were told, represented arguments from discussions of the same questions by peer groups). The higher the proportion of risky arguments, the greater the polarization in the direction of risk.
—Ebbe B. Ebbesen and Richard J. Bowers, Proportion of Risky to Conservative Arguments in a Group Discussion and Choice Shifts, *J. Personality & Soc. Psychol.* 29 (1974): 316, 317–27.

16. *Risk-taking in chess.* People were presented with the case of a low-ranked chess player debating whether to make a risky play against a high-ranked one. They were asked, as individuals, the lowest probability of success at which they would advise the player to make the risky play. Then they discussed the case in groups. The group consensus was more risk-inclined than the individual judgments.
—David G. Myers and Helmut Lamm, The Group Polarization Phenomenon, *Psychol. Bull.* 83 (1976): 602–7.

17. *Demand for money after deliberation.* People were asked to distribute eighteen profit units between themselves and another subject. They initially demanded, on average, 64 percent. After deliberation with

others (who were not competing for a share), the demand increased to
70 percent.
    —Helmut Lamm and Claudius Sauer, Discussion-Induced Shift toward
Higher Demands in Negotiation, *Eur. J. Soc. Psychol.* 4 (1974): 85, 85–88.

18. *Cautious shifts in racetrack betting.* Groups deliberating about racetrack bets
     were more cautious than individuals. The predeliberation inclination of
     individual bettors was to prefer favored horses over long shots; that
     inclination increased after deliberation.
         —Clark McCauley et al., Group Shift to Caution at the Race Track,
     J. Experimental Soc. Psychol. 98 (1973): 80, 80–86.

19. *Faculty evaluations.* Groups were presented with 200-word descriptions
     of "good" and "bad" faculty. After group discussion, the groups tended
     to rate the "good" faculty higher (and distribute them higher pay raises)
     than the mean of the individual judgment, while they rated "bad"
     faculty lower and were less likely to give them pay raises.
         —Myers, Attitude Comparison.

20. *Polarization of demands in labor negotiations.* Three-person union teams
     were given a hypothetical bargaining position that was either very strong
     or very weak, relative to the other party. In groups with a strong
     bargaining position, higher wages were demanded after discussion
     than the individuals' prediscussion positions. But in groups with weak
     bargaining positions, the groups were more conservative about their
     aspirations than they were as individuals.
         —Jacob M. Rabbie and Lieuwe Visser, Bargaining Strength and Group
     Polarization in Intergroup Negotiations, *Eur. J. Soc. Psychol.* 2 (1972):
     401–16.

21. *Risky shifts in professional decisions.* Eleven groups, each comprised of a
     psychiatrist, psychologist, and social worker, were presented with hypo-
     thetical choice dilemmas, half of a clinical nature, and half nonclinical.
     The groups evidenced a risky shift on all but one of the twelve items,
     and no significant difference was seen between the clinical and non-
     clinical items. (The presumed power of the psychiatrist was not signifi-
     cantly manifested in the group's decisions.)
         —Sheldon Siegel and Robert B. Zajonc, Group Risk Taking in Pro-
     fessional Decisions, *Sociometry* 30 (1967): 339, 339–49.

22. *Quantity of arguments presented.* The greater the number of arguments
     related to their initial position, the larger the shift, in the direction of
     either risk or caution.

—Eugene Burnstein et al., Interpersonal Comparison versus Persuasive Argumentation: A More Direct Test of Alternative Explanations for Group-Induced Shifts in Individual Choice, *J. Experimental Soc. Psychol.* 9 (1973): 236, 236–45.

23. *Group equity judgments of performers.* About 200 experimental subjects were asked to compare two performers and to divide a payment between them. There were two variables: whether the subjects anticipated future interaction with the performers and whether they made their judgments either individually or in groups of five. When future interaction was *not* expected, the result was simple: Individuals tended to allocate more money to the more productive performer, and in a group this effect was polarized, significantly increasing the percentage to be allocated to the more productive performer. When future interaction *was* expected, the result was intriguingly different: Individuals divided the money equally, while groups divided the money equitably, with more going to the more productive performer. In addition, people expressed more confidence about the fairness of the group consensus than about their individual judgments.
—Jerald Greenberg, Group vs Individual Equity Judgments: Is There a Polarization Effect? *J. Experimental Soc. Psychol.* 15 (1979): 504, 504–12.

24. *Polarization after hearing from a rival group.* People at a progressive French architecture school were asked to compare their schools with a more prestigious but more conservative school by first making judgments individually (on a scale from "strongly disagree" with the statement about the characteristic of the school to "strongly agree") and then coming up with a group consensus. Thereafter, people again made individual judgments. As would be expected, the postdiscussion responses reflected polarization. But here is an equally notable finding: After being confronted with the opinions of those at the rival school about their school, the students at the progressive school became even more polarized. This shift occurred both for items where they initially thought their school was superior, and for items where they initially thought the other school was superior. The introduction of a rival group's presumed opinion of one's own group therefore tends to polarize opinion still further.
—Willem Doise, Intergroup Relations and Polarization of Individual and Collective Judgments, *J. Personality & Soc. Psychol.* 12 (1969): 136, 136–43.

25. *Polarization toward novel arguments.* Participants were presented with arguments intended to produce risky or conservative shifts. The

arguments were rated by experimental subjects on two dimensions, as either valid or not valid and as either novel or not novel, and then the subjects were asked about the arguments' persuasiveness. The most persuasive arguments were both novel and of high validity. In addition, when confronted with two valid arguments, the subjects tended to polarize in the direction of the more novel one.

—Amiram Vinokur and Eugene Burnstein, Novel Argumentation and Attitude Change: The Case of Polarization Following Group Discussion, 8 *Eur. J. Soc. Psychol.* (1978): 335, 335–48.

26. *Militarism versus pacifism.* A large group of students was given an advance test on military-related issues, so that the group could be divided between "hawks" and "doves." Separated into those two groups, the subjects were asked to discuss and come to a consensus on a number of hypothetical military issues and were then given a postdiscussion individual evaluation. As expected, doves became more pacifist after discussion. Contrary to expectations, however, hawks became more pacifist as well. (The postdiscussion hawks, however, were still more hawkish than either the prediscussion or postdiscussion doves.) This surprising finding, for hawks, might be a product of rhetorical asymmetry: In the relevant group, social norms probably supported a shift toward pacifism.

—David G. Myers and Paul J. Bach, Discussion Effects on Militarism-Pacifism: A Test of the Group Polarization Hypothesis, *J. Personality & Soc. Psychol.* 30 (1974): 741, 741–47.

27. *Group polarization of the authoritarian juror.* About 280 students were classified as "high" or "low" authoritarians based on a survey and then asked to listen to a murder trial. The students were asked to judge the defendant's guilt and punishment and then placed in six-person juries. As expected, juries with high authoritarian jurors reached more guilty verdicts and sought harsher penalties than low authoritarian jurors. Moreover, the verdict change between prediscussion and post-discussion was more significant for high authoritarians than for low authoritarians.

—Robert M. Bray and Audrey M. Noble, Authoritarianism and Decisions of Mock Juries—Evidence of Jury Bias and Group Polarization, *J. Personality & Soc. Psychol.* 36 (1978): 1424, 1424–30.

28. *Polarization and age.* Participants from three age groups (adolescents, youths, and adults) were assessed either individually or with two peers of the same age for their risk preferences through a mix of questionnaires and a video game. The study found that those in peer groups made

riskier decisions than the individuals and also that group polarization decreased (but did not disappear) with age.

—Margo Gardner and Laurence Steinberg, Peer Influence on Risk Taking, Risk Preference, and Risky Decision Making in Adolescence and Adulthood: An Experimental Study, *Developmental Psychol.* 41 (2005): 625, 625–35.

Acknowledgments

I have been working on this topic for many years, and it is a pleasure to thank the many friends and colleagues who have helped. It is an understatement to say that the book could not have been done without them.

Thanks first to my coauthors on the various projects that have informed this book. On juries and punitive damages, I was privileged to work with Daniel Kahneman and David Schkade; the collaboration was amazingly instructive and great fun. On judicial voting, David Schkade was a fabulous collaborator, and my former students Lisa Ellman and Andres Sawicki were invaluable coauthors on the work that ultimately emerged. More recently, Thomas Miles and I have worked on several studies of judicial voting and regulatory policy. The Colorado study was a product of an experiment involving Reid Hastie and (yet again) David Schkade. On the theoretical foundations, I benefited from a wonderful collaboration with Edward Glaeser. I am more grateful than I can say to every one of these truly wonderful friends.

Over the years, I have also benefited from the comments, criticisms, and objections of many colleagues. For special thanks, I single out Martha Nussbaum for countless discussions, for unfailingly high standards, and for generous and invaluable help in getting the arguments straight. Thanks as well to Eric Posner, Richard Posner, Richard Thaler, and Adrian Vermeule—all terrific colleagues and friends, and people of truly extraordinary kindness and generosity. David McBride, my editor, provided support throughout and superb comments as well, greatly improving the book at the last stages. Special thanks finally to Jack Goldsmith, also a longtime colleague and friend, who took the trouble to read a near-final version of the book, and whose comments produced many improvements.

Special thanks are also due to the students in my freshman seminar on extremism at Harvard in the fall of 2008. Their intelligence, enthusiasm, and sheer inventiveness had a large impact on this book. I am most grateful to them.

My largest thanks go to my wife, Samantha Power. Samantha emphasized that in a book on extremism, it might not be a bad idea to talk about actual extremists and not to rest content with laboratory experiments. Her own experiences, her bravery, her curiosity, her energy, and her ideas greatly improved and deepened my discussion here. I am most grateful to her for that. But I am still more grateful to her for making the process of writing this book, and every day, such a joy.

Some sections of this book draw directly from some earlier work, including *Why Societies Need Dissent* (Cambridge, Mass.: Harvard University Press, 2003) and *Infotopia: How Many Minds Produce Knowledge* (New York: Oxford University Press, 2006). Some of the central ideas here were initially sketched in Deliberative Trouble? Why Groups Go to Extremes (*Yale L. J.* 110 (2000): 71). More recently, a 2007 lecture at the American Enterprise Institute was published as a short monograph, *Why Groups Go to*

Extremes (Washington, D.C.: American Enterprise Institute, 2008). I am especially grateful to the audience at AEI, above all, Chris DeMuth and Robert Hahn, for providing a stimulating forum at which many of the ideas here initially took shape.

Notes

Chapter 1

1. Serge Moscovici and Marisa Zavalloni, The Group as a Polarizer of Attitudes, *J. Personality & Soc. Psych.* 12 (1969): 125.
2. See Roger Brown, *Social Psychology: The Second Edition* (New York: Free Press, 1985), 203–226.
3. See Ibid., 204.
4. David G. Myers and George D. Bishop, Discussion Effects on Racial Attitudes, *Science* 169 (1970): 778–79.
5. David G. Myers, Discussion-Induced Attitude Polarization, *Hum. Rel.* 16 (1975): 699, 707–11 (finding increase in support for feminism among women inclined to show feminist attitudes).
6. See Albert Breton and Silvana Dalmazzone, Information Control, Loss of Autonomy, and the Emergence of Political Extremism, in *Political Extremism and Rationality* (Albert Bretton et al., eds., Cambridge: Cambridge University Press, 2002), 53–55.
7. See Marc Sageman, *Leaderless Jihad* (Philadelphia: University of Pennsylvania Press, 2008).
8. See Reid Hastie, David Schkade, and Cass R. Sunstein, What Happened on Deliberation Day? *Cal. L. Rev* 95 (2007): 915
9. These examples are taken from Cass R. Sunstein et al., *Are Judges Political? An Empirical Investigation* (Washington, D.C.: Brookings, 2005).
10. See Cass R. Sunstein et al., *Punitive Damages: How Juries Decide* (Chicago: University of Chicago Press, 2007).
11. See James A. F. Stoner, A Comparison of Individual and Group Decisions Involving Risk (July 31, 1961) (unpublished MS thesis, Massachusetts Institute of Technology), on file with the Massachusetts Institute of Technology Library, available at http://hdl.handle.net/1721.1/11330.

12. See Lawrence Hong, Risky Shift and Cautious Shift: Some Direct Evidence on the Culture Value Theory, *Social Psych.* 41 (1978): 342.

13. See ibid.

14. Moscovici and Zavalloni, The Group as a Polarizer of Attitudes.

15. Ibid.; Brown, *Social Psychology*, 210–12.

16. See Hong, Risky Shift and Cautious Shift.

17. John C. Turner et al., *Rediscovering the Social Group:* A Self-Categorization Theory 142–170 (New York: Basil Blackwell, 1987).

18. Ibid., 153.

19. Ibid.

20. Paul Cromwell et al., Group Effects on Decision-Making by Burglars, *Psychol. Rep.* 69 (1991): 579, 586.

21. Norbert L. Kerr et al., Bias in Judgment: Comparing Individuals and Groups, *Psychol. Rev.* 103 (1996): 687, 689, 691–93 (citing studies).

22. See Norris Johnson et al., Crowd Behavior as "Risky Shift": A Laboratory Experiment, *Sociometry* 40 (1977): 183.

23. Ibid., 186.

24. See E. Allan Lind et al., The Social Construction of Injustice: Fairness Judgments in Response to Own and Others' Unfair Treatment by Authorities, *Organizational Behavior and Human Decision Processes* 75 (1998): 1.

25. Ibid., 16.

Chapter 2

1. See Brown, *Social Psychology*, 200–45.

2. See Robert Baron et al., Social Corroboration and Opinion Extremity, *J. Experimental Soc. Psych.* 32 (1996): 537.

3. See Mark Kelman et al., Context-Dependence in Legal Decision Making, *J. Legal Stud.* 25 (1996): 287, 287–88.

4. Baron et al., Social Corroboration.

5. See Chip Heath and Richard Gonzales, Interaction with Others Increases Decision Confidence but Not Decision Quality: Evidence against Information Collection Views of Interactive Decision Making, *Organizational Behavior and Human Decision Processes* 61 (1997): 305–26.

6. See Sageman, *Leaderless Jihad.*

7. Ibid., 116.

8. Ibid.

9. See Joseph Henrich et al., Group Report: What Is the Role of Culture in Bounded Rationality? in *Bounded Rationality: The Adaptive Toolbox* (Gerd Gigerenzer and Reinhard Selten, eds., Cambridge, Mass.: MIT Press, 2001), 353–54, for an entertaining outline in connection with food choice decisions.

10. Edward Glaeser, Psychology and Paternalism, *U. Chi. L. Rev.* 73 (2006): 133.

11. It has similarly been suggested that majorities are especially potent because people do not want to incur the wrath, or lose the favor, of large numbers of people, and that when minorities have influence, it is because they produce genuine attitudinal change. See Baron et al., Social Corroboration, 82.

12. Ibid.

13. Cecilia L. Ridgeway, Social Status and Group Structure, in *Group Processes* (Michael A. Hogg and R. Scott Tindale, eds., 2001), 352, 354 (collecting studies).

14. See Gwen M. Wittenbaum et al., Mutual Enhancement toward an Understanding of the Collective Preference for Shared Information, *J. Personality & Soc. Psych.* 77 (1999): 967, 967–78.

15. See Scott McClellan, *What Happened* (New York: Public Affairs, 2008).

16. Ibid., 253.

17. See Doris Kearns Goodwin, *Team of Rivals* (New York: Simon & Schuster, 2005).

18. Jean Hatzfeld, *Machete Season* (New York: Farrar, Straus & Giroux, 2005), 71.

19. Ibid., 38.

20. See Timur Kuran, *Public Lies, Private Truths* (Cambridge: Harvard University Press, 1998).

21. Catherine Hafer and Dimitri Landa, Deliberation as Self-Discovery and Institutions for Political Speech, *J. Theoretical Politics* 19 (2007): 329.

22. Ibid.

23. For a formal discussion, see Edward L. Glaeser and Cass R. Sunstein, Extremism and Social Learning, *J. Legal Analysis* (forthcoming 2009).

24. See Russell Hardin, The Crippled Epistemology of Extremism, in *Political Rationality and Extremism* (Albert Breton et al., eds., Cambridge: Cambridge University Press, 2002).

25. See Glaeser and Sunstein, Extremism and Social Learning.

26. See http://www.orgnet.com/divided.html.

27. The best discussion is Henry Farrell et al., Self-Segregation or Deliberation? Blog Readership, Participation, and Polarization in American Politics (unpublished manuscript 2008).

28. See Bill Bishop, *The Big Sort: Why the Clustering of Like Minded America Is Tearing Us Apart* (New York: Houghton Mifflin, 2007).

29. See David Schkade et al., Deliberating about Dollars: The Severity Shift, *Colum. L. Rev.* 100 (2000): 1139, 1152, 1155–56.

30. Ibid., 1161–62.

31. See Caryn Christensen and Ann S. Abbott, Team Medical Decision Making, in *Decision Making in Health Care* (Gretchen B. Chapman and Frank A. Sonnenberg, eds., Cambridge: Cambridge University Press, 2000), 267, 269, 272–76 (discussing effects of status on exchange of information in group interactions).

32. Timothy Cason and Vai-Lam Mui, A Laboratory Study of Group Polarisation in the Team Dictator Game, *Econ. J.* 107 (1997): 1465.

33. See ibid.

34. Ibid., 1468–72.

35. This is a lesson of the study of punitive damage awards, where groups with extreme medians showed the largest shifts; see Schkade et al., Deliberating about Dollars, 1152. For other evidence, see Turner et al., *Rediscovering the Social Group*, 158.

36. See Maryla Zaleska, The Stability of Extreme and Moderate Responses in Different Situations, in *Group Decision Making* (H. Brandstetter, J. H. Davis, and G. Stocker-Kreichgauer, eds., London: Academic Press, 1982), 163, 164.

37. See Russell Hardin, The Crippled Epistemology of Extremism, in *Political Rationality and Extremism* (Albert Breton et al., eds., Cambridge: Cambridge University Press, 2002), 3, 16.

38. See Scott McClellan, *What Happened*.

39. Dominic Abrams et al., Knowing What to Think by Knowing Who You Are, *Br. J. Soc. Psych.* 29 (1990): 97, 112.

40. See John Turner et al., *Rediscovering the Social Group* (London: Blackwell, 1987), 154–59, which attempts to use this evidence as a basis for a synthesis, called "a self-categorization theory of group polarization" (154).

41. Russell Spears, Martin Lee, and Stephen Lee, De-Individuation and Group Polarization in Computer-Mediated Communication, *Br. J. Soc. Psych.* 29 (1990): 121.

42. Abrams et al., Knowing What to Think.

43. Sageman, *Leaderless Jihad*.

44. Albert Hirschman, *Exit, Voice, and Loyalty: Responses to Decline in Firms, Organizations, and States* (Cambridge, Mass.: Harvard University Press, 1972).

45. Ibid., 46.

46. For detailed discussion, see Cass R. Sunstein, *Infotopia* (New York: Oxford University Press, 2006).

47. R. L. Thorndike, The Effect of Discussion upon the Correctness of Group Decisions, When the Factor of Majority Influence Is Allowed For, *J. Soc. Psych.* 9 (1938): 343.

48. See H. Burnstein, Persuasion as Argument Processing, in *Group Decision Making*, Brandstetter et al., eds.

49. Brown, *Social Psychology*, 225.

50. See L. Ross, M. R. Lepper, and M. Hubbard, Perseverance in Self-Perception and Social Perception: Biased Attributional Processes in the Debriefing Paradigm," *J. Personality & Soc. Psych.* 32 (1975): 880–92; Dan Kahan et al., Biased Assimilation, Polarization, and Cultural Credibility: An Experimental Study of Nanotechnology Risk Perceptions (unpublished manuscript, 2008).

51. See ibid.; Geoffret Munro and Peter Ditto, Biased Assimilation, Attitude Polarization, and Affect in Reactions to Stereotype-Relevant Scientific Information, *J. Personality & Soc. Psych.* 23 (1997): 636.

52. See Brendan Nyhan and Jason Reifler, When Corrections Fail: The Persistence of Political Misperceptions (unpublished manuscript, 2008).

53. Sageman, *Leaderless Jihad*, 99.

54. Ibid.

55. See James S. Fishkin, *The Voice of the People: Public Opinion and Democracy* (New Haven, Conn.: Yale University Press, 1995).

56. Ibid., 206–7.

57. James S. Fishkin and Robert C. Luskin, Bringing Deliberation to the Democratic Dialogue, in *The Poll with a Human Face* (Maxwell McCombs and Amy Reynolds, eds., (New York: Lawrence Erlbaum, 1999), 3, 29, 31.

58. See ibid., 22–23 (showing a jump, on a scale of 1 to 4, from 3.51 to 3.58 in intensity of commitment to reducing the deficit); a jump, on a scale of 1 to 3, from 2.71 to 2.85 in intensity of support for greater spending on education; showing a jump, on a scale of 1 to 3, from 1.95 to 2.16, in commitment to aiding American business interests abroad).

59. Ibid., 23. See also ibid., 22 (showing an increase, on a scale of 1 to 3, from 1.40 to 1.59, in commitment to spending on foreign aid; also showing a decrease, on a scale of 1 to 3, from 2.38 to 2.27, in commitment to spending on Social Security).

60. See Brown, *Social Psychology*.

61. See James Miller, *Democracy Is in the Streets* (Cambridge, Mass.: Harvard University Press, 1994).

62. See Sageman, *Leaderless Jihad*.

63. Valuable discussions are Kuran, *Public Lies, Private Truths*; Marc Granovetter, Threshold Models of Collective Behavior, *Am. J. Soc.* 83 (1978): 1420.

64. See Kuran, *Public Lies, Private Truths*.

65. See ibid.; Susanne Lohmann, The Dynamics of Informational Cascades, *World Politics* 47 (1994): 42; Susanne Lohmann, Collective Action Cascades: An Informational Rationale for the Power in Numbers, *Journal of Economic Surveys* 14 (2000): 655.

66. See Stanley Milgram, *Obedience to Authority* (Princeton, N.J.: Princeton University Press, 1974); Stanley Milgram, Behavioral Study of Obedience, in *Readings about the Social Animal* (Elliott Aronson, ed., New York: W. H. Freeman, 1995), 23.

67. Milgram, Behavioral Study of Obedience, 27.

68. Ibid., 29.

69. Ibid., 30.

70. See Milgram, *Obedience to Authority*.

71. Ibid., 23.

72. Ibid.

73. Ibid., 55–57.

74. Ibid., 34.

75. This unconventional interpretation is set out in Thomas Blass, The Milgram Paradigm after 35 Years: Some Things We Now Know about Obedience to Authority, in *Obedience to Authority: Critical Perspectives on the Milgram Paradigm*

(Thomas Blass, ed., New York: Lawrence Erlbaum Associates, 1999), 35, 38–44; Robert Shiller, *The Subprime Crisis* (Princeton, N.J.: Princeton University Press, 2008), 150–51.

76. Blass, The Milgram Paradigm, 42–44.

77. Milgram, *Obedience to Authority*, 113–22.

78. Ibid.

79. See Philip Zimbardo, *The Lucifer Effect* (New York: Random House, 2007).

80. Ibid.

81. Ibid.

82. See ibid.

83. See Hatzfeld, *Machete Season*, 71–72.

84. Ibid., 74.

85. Tzvetan Todorov, *Facing the Extreme* (Holt: New York, 1996), 123.

86. Ibid., 123–24.

87. See Zimbardo, *The Lucifer Effect*.

88. Ibid., 396.

89. Ibid.

90. Ibid.

91. Quoted from a 1979 television interview in Robert V. Levine, Milgram's Progress, American Scientist Online, July–August 2004.

92. See Philip Gourevitch and Errol Morris, *Standard Operating Procedure* (New York: Penguin, 2008).

93. Ibid., 117.

94. Ibid., 211.

95. Quoted in Zimbardo, *The Lucifer Effect*, 15.

96. Gourevitch and Morris, *Standard Operating Procedure*, 100.

97. Ibid.

98. See ibid., 166–67.

99. See Hatzfeld, *Machete Season*, 50.

100. I discuss the question in Cass R. Sunstein, *Republic.com 2.0* (Princeton, N. J.: Princeton University Press, 2007).

101. See Arnold Jacobs, *Race, Media, and the Crisis of Civil Society* (Cambridge: Cambridge University Press, 2001), 144.

102. Sageman, *Leaderless Jihad*.

103. See Patricia Wallace, *The Psychology of the Internet* (Cambridge: Cambridge University Press, 2000), 73–84.

104. Sageman, *Leaderless Jihad*, 121.

105. Ibid.

106. Ibid.

107. Ibid., 123.

108. See Miller McPherson et al., Birds of a Feather: Homophily in Social Networks, *Annu. Rev. Soc.* 27 (2001): 415.

109. Ibid., 429

110. Ibid., 425.

111. See Noah Mark, Culture and Competition: Homophily and Distancing Explanations for Cultural Niches, *Am. Soc. Rev.* 68 (2003): 319.

112. Ibid., 326.

113. See Irving Janis, *Groupthink* (2nd ed.) (Boston: Houghton Mifflin, 1982).

114. Ibid., 198–241.

115. Ibid., 187–91.

116. Marlene Turner and Anthony Pratkanis, Twenty Years of Groupthink Theory and Research: Lessons from the Evaluation of a Theory, *Organizational Behavioral and Human Decision Processes* 73 (1998): 105, 107.

117. See Scott McClellan, *What Happened*.

118. Ibid., 175.

119. Ibid., 174–75.

120. Ibid., 262–71.

121. James Esser, Alive and Well after Twenty-Five Years: A Review of Groupthink Research, *Organizational Behavior and Human Decision Processes* 73 (1998): 116.

122. See Sally Riggs Fuller and Ramon J. Aldag, *Organizational Behavior and Human Decision Processes* 73 (1998): 163

123. Ibid., 167.

124. Randall Peterson et al., Group Dynamics in Top Management Teams: Groupthink, Vigilance, and Alternative Models of Organizational Failure and Success, *Journal of Organizational Behavior and Human Decision Processes* 73 (1998): 272.

125. Ibid., 278.

126. See Esser, Alive and Well, 118–122.

127. Philip Tetlock et al., Assessing Political Group Dynamics, *J. Personality & Soc. Psych.* 63 (1992): 781.

128. Esser, Alive and Well, 130–31.

129. Ibid., 131.

130. Ibid., 131–32.

131. Ibid., 132.

132. See Shiller, *The Subprime Crisis*.

133. I draw here on David Hirshleifer, The Blind Leading the Blind: Social Influence, Fads, and Informational Cascades, in *The New Economics of Human Behavior* (Mariano Tommasi and Kathryn Ierulli, eds., Cambridge: Cambridge University Press, 1995), 188, 193–95; and on the discussion in Cass R. Sunstein, *Why Societies Need Dissent* (Cambridge, Mass.: Harvard University Press, 2003), 55–73.

134. See Shiller, *The Subprime Crisis*.

135. See Matthew J. Salganik et al., "Experimental Study of Inequality and Unpredictability in an Artificial Cultural Market," *Science* 311 (2006).

136. See Fabio Lorenzi-Cioldi and Alain Clémence, Group Processes and the Construction of Social Representations, in *Group Processes*, Hogg and Tindale, eds., 311, 315–17.

137. See Duncan Watts, *The Kerry Cascade*, available at http://slate.msn.com/id/2095993/.

Chapter 3

1. See Sharon Groch, Free Spaces: Creating Oppositional Spaces in the Disability Rights Movement, in *Oppositional Consciousness* (Jane Mansbridge and Aldon Morris, eds., Chicago: University of Chicago Press, 2001), 65, 67–72.

2. See ibid., 95.

3. See Dennis Chong, *Collective Action and the Civil Rights Movement* (Chicago: University of Chicago Press, 1991).

4. See Brooke Harrington, *Pop Finance* (Princeton, N.J.: Princeton University Press, 2008).

5. See Robert Shiller, *Irrational Exuberance* (Princeton, N.J.: Princeton University Press, 2000); Robert Shiller, *The Subprime Solution* (Princeton, N.J.: Princeton University Press, 2008).

6. Shiller, *The Subprime Solution*, 41.

7. Ibid., 46.

8. See Robert Shiller, *Irrational Exuberance*, 2nd ed. (Princeton, N.J.: Princeton University Press, 2004).

9. See Robert Shiller, How the Bubble Stayed under the Radar, *New York Times*, March 2, 2008, available at http://www.nytimes.com/2008/03/02/business/02view.html?ex=1362114000&en=f450ee18dc5cde60&ei=5124&partner=permalink&exprod=permalink.

10. See Gordon Wood, *The Radicalism of the American Revolution* (New York: Vintage, 1993).

11. For fascinating studies, see Arnold Dashefsky, *Ethnic Identification among American Jews* (Washington, D.C.: University Press of America, 1993); Flore Zéphir, *Trends in Ethnic Identification among Second-Generation Haitian Immigrants in New York City* (Westport, Conn: Bergin & Garvey, 2001).

12. See Timur Kuran, Ethnic Norms and Their Transformation through Reputational Cascades, *J. Legal Stud.* 27 (1998): 623.

13. Ibid.

14. I draw here on Cass R. Sunstein and Adrian Vermeule, Conspiracy Theories: Causes and Cures, *J. Polit. Phil.* (forthcoming 2009).

15. See Richard Hofstadter, The Paranoid Style in American Politics, in *The Paranoid Style in American Politics and Other Essays* (New York: Vintage, 2008); Robert S. Robins and Jerrold M. Post, *Political Paranoia: The Psychopolitics of*

Hatred (New Haven, Conn.: Yale University Press, 1997). Another common idea treats conspiracy theories as a form of collective paranoid delusion.

16. Russell Hardin, The Crippled Epistemology of Extremism, in *Political Rationality and Extremism* (Albert Breton et al., eds., Cambridge: Cambridge University Press, 2002), 3, 16.

17. Ibid. Of course, it is also true that many extremists have become extreme, or stayed extreme, after being exposed to a great deal of information on various sides.

18. See Alan Krueger, *What Makes a Terrorist?* (Princeton, N.J.: Princeton University Press, 2006), 75–82.

19. See ibid., 89–90.

20. See, for example, James Fetzer, *The 9/11 Conspiracy* (Chicago: Open Court, 2007); Mathias Broeckers, *Conspiracies, Conspiracy Theories, and the Secrets of 9/11* (Joshua Tree, Calif.: Progressive, 2006). The latter book sold more than 100,000 copies in Germany.

21. See Diane Goldstein, *Once upon a Virus* (Salt Lake City: University of Utah Press, 2004).

22. See Leon Festinger, *A Theory of Cognitive Dissonance* (Stanford, Calif.: Stanford University Press, 1957).

23. For a classic case study, see Leon Festinger et al., *When Prophecy Fails* (Minneapolis: University of Minnesota Press, 1956). For a general treatment, see Carol Tavris and Elliot Aronson, *Mistakes Were Made (but Not by Me)* (New York: Harvest, 2007).

24. For general discussion of the importance of thresholds, see Marc Granovetter, Threshold Models of Collective Behavior, *Am. J. Soc.* 83 (1978): 1420.

25. See Robert Repetto, ed., *Punctuated Equilibrium and the Dynamics of U.S. Environmental Policy* (New Haven, Conn.: Yale University Press, 2006); Timur Kuran and Cass R. Sunstein, Availability Cascades and Risk Regulation, *Stan. L. Rev.* 51 (1999): 683.

26. See Chip Heath, Chris Bell, and Emily Sternberg, Emotional Selection in Memes: The Case of Urban Legends, *J. Personality & Soc. Psych.* 81 (2001): 1028.

27. Ibid., 1037–39.

28. Ibid., 1039.

29. Ibid., 1040.

30. Ibid., 1041.

31. See Cass R. Sunstein, Some Thoughts on Indignation and Law, *Vermont L. Rev.* (forthcoming 2009).

32. See Cass R. Sunstein et al., *Punitive Damages: How Juries Decide* (Chicago: University of Chicago Press, 2002), 32–33.

33. See Schkade et al., Deliberating about Dollars, 1152, showing that in the top five outrage cases, the mean shift was 11 percent, higher than in any other class of cases. The effect is more dramatic still for dollars (see ibid.), where high

dollar awards shifted upward by a significant margin. This finding is closely connected to another one: Extremists are most likely to shift, and likely to shift most, as a result of discussions with one another. See John Turner et al., *Rediscovering the Social Group* (London: Blackwell, 1987), 154–59.

34. See Krueger, *What Makes a Terrorist?* and Sageman, *Leaderless Jihad.*

35. See Sageman, *Leaderless Jihad.*

36. See Krueger, *What Makes a Terrorist?*

37. See Sageman, *Leaderless Jihad.*

38. Ibid.

39. Giles Foden, Secrets of a Terror Merchant, *Melbourne Age,* September 14, 2001.

40. Jeffeey Bartholet, Method to the Madness, *Newsweek,* October 22, 2001, 55.

41. Stephen Grey and Dipesh Gadher, Inside Bin Laden's Academies of Terror, *Sunday Times* (London), October 7, 2001, 10.

42. Vithal C. Nadkarni, How to Win over Foes and Influence Their Minds, *Times of India,* October 7, 2001.

43. See Sageman, *Leaderless Jihad,* 69.

44. Ibid.

45. Ibid.

46. Ibid.

47. Ibid., 87.

48. See Hardin, The Crippled Epistemology of Extremism.

49. Ibid., 11.

50. See Glaeser and Sunstein, Extremism and Social Learning.

51. See Robert Pape, The Strategic Logic of Suicide Terrorism, *Am. Polit. Sci. Rev.* 97 (2003): 1; Robert Pape, *Dying to Win: The Strategic Logic of Suicide Terrorism* (Chicago: University of Chicago Press, 2006).

52. Pape, The Strategic Logic of Suicide Terrorism, 2.

53. Ibid.

54. See Harrington, *Pop Finance.*

55. See Janis, *Groupthink.*

56. See Ronald Wintrobe, *Rational Extremism* (Cambridge: Cambridge University Press, 2007).

57. See Neil Weinstein, Unrealistic Optimism about Future Life Events, *J. Personality and Soc. Psych.* 39 (1980): 806.

58. See Shelley Taylor, *Positive Illusions* (New York: Basic Books, 1991), 10.

59. See Dominic Johnson, *Overconfidence and War: The Havoc and Glory of Positive Illusions* (Cambridge, Mass.: Harvard University Press, 2006).

60. See Kuran and Sunstein, Availability Cascades, 683.

61. Paul Slovic, *The Perception of Risk* (London; Sterling, Va.: Earthscan, 2000), 40.

Chapter 4

1. Edmund Burke, Reflections on the Revolution in France, in *The Portable Edmund Burke* (Isaac Kramnick, ed., New York: Penguin, 1999), 442.

2. Ibid., 451.

3. Ibid., 428.

4. Ibid., 451.

5. Ibid.

6. Ibid.

7. See Gregory Moschetti, Individual Maintenance and Perpetuation of a Means-Ends Arbitrary Tradition, *Sociometry* 40 (1977): 78.

8. See Timur Kuran, *Private Truths, Public Lies* (Cambridge, Mass.: Harvard University Press, 1998).

9. For discussion, see Cass R. Sunstein, *A Constitution of Many Minds* (Princeton, N.J.: Princeton University Press, 2009, forthcoming).

10. Ibid., No. 14 (James Madison), 72.

11. Ibid.

12. Letter from Thomas Jefferson to Samuel Kercheval (July 12, 1816), in *The Portable Thomas Jefferson* (Merrill D. Peterson, ed., New York: Penguin, 1975), 552, 559. Note, however, that Jefferson is speaking of experience, not of a priori reasoning (or "book-reading").

13. Blaise Pascal, Preface to the Treatise on Vacuum, in *Thoughts, Letters, and Minor Works* (Charles W. Eliot, ed., M. L. Booth et al., trans., Cambridge, Mass.: Harvard University Press 1910), 444, 449.

14. Jeremy Bentham, *Handbook of Political Fallacies* 43–53 (Harold Larabee ed., New York: Octagon Books, 1952)

15. Ibid., 44.

16. Ibid., 45.

17. See Dan Kahan, The Secret Ambition of Deterrence, *Harv. L. Rev.* 113 (1999): 413.

18. Ibid.

19. See Cass R. Sunstein, *Risk and Reason* (New York: Cambridge University Press, 2000).

20. See Matthew Adler and Eric Posner, *New Foundations for Cost-Benefit Analysis* (Cambridge, Mass.: Harvard University Press, 2006); Sunstein, *Risk and Reason.*

21. A focal point of such disputes is Nicholas Stern, *The Economics of Climate Change* (Cambridge: Cambridge University Press, 2007).

22. See William Nordhaus, *The Challenge of Global Warming: Economic Models and Environmental Policy* (New Haven, Conn.: Yale University Press, 2008); a dated but still helpful treatment is William Nordhaus and Joseph Boyer, *Warming the World* (New Haven, Conn.: Yale University Press, 2000).

23. *The Complete Antifederalist* (H. Storing, ed., Chicago: University of Chicago Press, 1980), 2:269.

24. [Alexander Hamilton], The Federalist No. 70, in *The Federalist Papers* (Clinton Rossiter, ed., New York: Signet, 1961), 426–37. Compare Asch's claim: "The clash of views generates events of far-reaching importance. I am induced to take up a particular standpoint, to view my own action as another views it. . . . Now I have within me two standpoints, my own and that of the other; both are now part of my way of thinking. In this way the limitations of my individual thinking are transcended by including the thoughts of others. I am now open." See Solomon Asch, *Social Psychology* (New York: Prentice-Hall, 1952), 131–32. From a quite different discipline, John Rawls writes in similar terms: "In everyday life the exchange of opinion with others checks our partiality and widens our perspective; we are made to see things from the standpoint of others and the limits of our vision are brought home to us. . . . The benefits from discussion lie in the fact that even representative legislators are limited in knowledge and the ability to reason. No one of them knows everything the others know, or can make all the same inferences that they can draw in concert. Discussion is a way of combining information and enlarging the range of arguments." See John Rawls, *A Theory of Justice* (Cambridge, Mass.: Harvard University Press, 1971), 358–59. The idea can be traced to Aristotle, suggesting that when diverse groups "all come together . . . they may surpass—collectively and as a body, although not individually—the quality of the few best. . . . When there are many who contribute to the process of deliberation, each can bring his share of goodness and moral prudence; . . . some appreciate one part, some another, and all together appreciate all." See Aristotle, *The Politics of Aristotle* (E. Barker, trans., London: Oxford University Press, 1972), 123. Much of my discussion here has been devoted to showing why and under what circumstances this view might or might not be true.

25. Max Farrand, ed., *The Records of the Federal Convention of 1787* (New Haven, Conn.: Yale University Press, 1966), 3:21, 359.

26. James Wilson, Lectures on Law, in *The Works of James Wilson* (Robert Green McCloskey, ed., Cambridge, Mass.: Harvard University Press, 1967), 1:291.

27. See The Pocket Veto Case, 279 U.S. 655, 678 (1929) (contending that it is an "essential . . . part of the constitutional provisions, guarding against ill-considered and unwise legislation, that the President . . . should have the full time allowed him for determining whether he should approve or disapprove a bill, and if disapproved, for adequately formulating the objections that should be considered by Congress"); *The Works of James Wilson*, 1:290, 432 (urging that the president's qualified veto will "secure an additional degree of accuracy and circumspection in the manner of passing the laws").

28. U.S. Const., Art. 1, section 8, clause 11.

29. Philip Kurland and Ralph Lerner, eds., *The Founders' Constitution* (Chicago: University of Chicago Press, 1992), 94.

30. Ibid.

31. Ibid.

32. Ibid.

33. See Vincent Blasi, The Checking Value in First Amendment Theory, *American Bar Association Research Journal* 2 (1977): 523.

34. Sageman, *Leaderless Jihad*, 160.

35. Ibid.

36. See, for example, Jon Elster, ed., *Deliberative Democracy* (Cambridge: Cambridge University Press, 1997).

37. See Scott Page, *The Difference* (Princeton, N.J.: Princeton University Press, 2007); Cass R. Sunstein, *Infotopia* (New York: Oxford University Press, 2006).

38. See William P. Bottom et al., Propagation of Individual Bias through Group Judgment: Error in the Treatment of Asymmetrically Informative Signals, *J. Risk & Uncertainty* 25 (2002): 147, 152–54.

39. For the arithmetic: Suppose that a group has N voters, and that they are choosing between two alternatives. Each voter has the same probability, p, of being right, with p being somewhere between 50 percent and 100 percent. Assume, too, that each group member has the same probability of making an accurate decision, and that each member's judgment is statistically independent. The probability, p/N, that the group will reach the right decision by majority rule is captured in this way:

$$P_n = \sum_{h\,(n+1)/2}^{n} [n!/h!(n-h)!]p^h(1-p)^{n-h}$$

I draw here on Dennis C. Mueller, *Public Choice III* (Cambridge: Cambridge University Press, 2003), 129; Robert E. Goodin, *Reflective Democracy* (Oxford: Oxford University Press, 2005), 95–96. Thanks to David Weisbach for help.

40. Condorcet, *Selected Writings* (Keith Michael Baker, ed., Indianapolis: Bobbs-Merrill, 1976), 62. This point is emphasized in David Estlund, *Democratic Authority: A Philosophical Framework* (Princeton, N.J.: Princeton University Press, 2007).

41. See Page, *The Difference*.

42. Luther Gulick, *Administrative Reflections from World War II* (New York: Greenwood, 1948).

43. Ibid., 120.

44. Ibid., 121.

45. Ibid., 125.

46. Ibid.

47. Ibid.

48. Ibid.

49. See Dan Reiter and Allan Stam, *Democracies at War* (Princeton, N.J.: Princeton University Press, 2002).

50. Caryn Christensen and Ann S. Abbott, Team Medical Decision Making, in *Decision Making in Health Care* (Gretchen B. Chapman and Frank A. Sonnenberg, eds., Cambridge: Cambridge University Press, 2000), 267, 272–76 (discussing effects of status on exchange of information in group interactions).

51. Jeffrey A. Sonnenfeld, What Makes Great Boards Great, *Harvard Business Review* (September 2002).

Chapter 5

1. See Heather Gerken, Second-Order Diversity and Disaggregated Democracy, *Harv. L. Rev.* 118 (2005): 1099.

2. For a superb discussion, see Elizabeth Anderson, John Stuart Mill and Experiments in Living, *Ethics* 102 (1991): 2.

3. See the important discussion in Diana Mutz, *Hearing the Other Side* (Cambridge: Cambridge University Press, 2006).

4. See Christenson and Abbott, Team Medical Decision Making, 273.

5. Ibid., 274.

6. C. Kirchmeyer and A. Cohen, Multicultural Groups: Their Performance and Reactions with Constructive Conflict, *Group and Organization Management* 17 (1992): 153.

7. See Letter to Madison (January 30, 1798), reprinted in *The Portable Thomas Jefferson* (M. Peterson, ed., New York: Viking, 1975), 882.

8. *Hague v. CIO*, 307 US 496 (1939). For present purposes, it is not necessary to discuss the public forum doctrine in detail. Interested readers might consult Geoffrey Stone et al., *The First Amendment* (Boston: Aspen, 1999), 286–330.

9. See the excellent discussion in Noah D. Zatz, Sidewalks in Cyberspace: Making Space for Public Forums in the Electronic Environment, *Harv. J. Law & Tech.* 12 (1998): 149.

10. See Kathleen Hall Jamieson and Joseph Capella, *Echo Chamber* (New York: Oxford University Press, 2008).

11. See Sunstein and Vermeule, Conspiracy Theories.

12. See Sonnenfeld, What Makes Great Boards Great; Harrington, *Pop Finance*.

Index